T0366999

LEARNING FROM WORK

ANNE BEAMISH

Learning from Work

Designing Organizations for Learning and Communication

STANFORD BUSINESS BOOKS

AN IMPRINT OF STANFORD UNIVERSITY PRESS

STANFORD, CALIFORNIA

Stanford University Press
Stanford, California

©2008 by the Board of Trustees of the
Leland Stanford Junior University.
All rights reserved.

Based on *Creating Communities of Practice*, a dissertation for the
Department of Urban Studies and Planning, School of Architecture
and Planning at MIT. Copyright © 2000 by the Massachusetts Institute
of Technology. Reprinted by permission.

This book has been published with the assistance of a University
Co-operative Society Subvention Grant awarded by The University
of Texas at Austin.

No part of this book may be reproduced or transmitted in any form or
by any means, electronic or mechanical, including photocopying and
recording, or in any information storage or retrieval system without the
prior written permission of Stanford University Press.

Printed in the United States of America
on acid-free, archival-quality paper

Library of Congress Cataloging-in-Publication Data
Beamish, Anne, date
  Learning from work : designing organizations for learning and
communication / Anne Beamish.
      p. cm.
  Includes bibliographical references and index.
  ISBN 978-0-8047-5715-7 (cloth : alk. paper)—ISBN 978-0-8047-5716-4
(pbk. : alk. paper)
  1. Knowledge management. 2. Work environment. 3. Organizational
behavior. 4. Interpersonal relations. 5. Automobile dealers—United
States—Case studies. I. Title.
HD30.2B42 2008
658.4'038—dc22
                                                    2007031386

Typeset by Classic Typography in 10/14 Janson

Contents

Figures and Tables

Acknowledgments

I have benefited enormously from the advice, support, and involvement of many individuals, and this book could not have been completed without their help.

First, I consider myself very fortunate to have studied under William J. Mitchell, Frank Levy, Lawrence Vale, Sherry Turkle, and Donald A. Schön while a graduate student at MIT. A significant part of the original research for this book was done while I was there, and their insight, guidance, and advice over the years have been invaluable. I'm also very appreciative of Sarah Kuhn and Starling David Hunter III, whose thoughtful reviews and very good suggestions made this a much stronger book. In spite of all this superb guidance, I of course take sole responsibility for any errors of fact, omission, or interpretation.

I would like to thank Geoffrey Burn and the staff of the Stanford University Press for their work and commitment to this manuscript, as well as David Horne of Classic Typography and Colleen Daly of Derbydog Industries for their extremely helpful editing.

I am especially grateful to the employees of "Northeastern Motors," who good-naturedly tolerated my questions and presence in their midst. Without their help, patience, and candid opinions, this book would never have been written.

I'd like to thank Dean Fritz Steiner and my colleagues in the School of Architecture at The University of Texas at Austin. It has been a privilege and pleasure working with them over the past five years. Friends have also played an important role and deserve special recognition for their friendship, encouragement, and camaraderie, especially Peg, Joanne, Lee, Barbara, and Susan.

I'd also like to acknowledge the generous support of The University of Texas at Austin for awarding a University Co-operative Society Subvention Grant to publish this book.

And finally, I'd like to thank my family. As always, my greatest debt is to my husband, Will Donovan. His constant support and encouragement over the years have meant everything.

Thank you all.

CHAPTER ONE

Introduction

Millions of Americans bought or serviced a vehicle during the past year, and for most the experience was not particularly pleasurable. The automobile dealership is an institution that has been with us for generations and plays an import role in our economy and our culture. The vehicles themselves are objects that we covet. They announce to the world who we are and who we aspire to be. Vans, sports cars, SUVs, hybrids, and trucks all speak volumes about the identities and lifestyles of their owners. The experience of owning a vehicle is not a problem, but buying or maintaining one certainly can be. Buying a car is a prospect dreaded by most customers, nicely summarized in the titles of books, magazine articles, and videotapes on the subject: "How to Buy a Car: Beating the Sales People at Their Game," *I'm a Legal Hold Up Man, I'm a Car Salesman,* and *Kicking Tires Virtually*—"Your days of being double-teamed by sleazy salesmen in white alligator shoes are over: Here's how to buy a car on the Internet." Though Americans may love cars, the process of buying one can be unpleasant.

This book is about a type of workplace—automobile dealerships—and the work that is done there, the people who work in them, and, most important, how dealership employees learn and communicate with each other, with customers, and with colleagues in the head office. Though dealerships may be familiar to most of us, as workplaces they are far more complex than the average customer would ever suspect. Even car dealers' negative behavior begins to make sense when viewed in the context of their social and cultural, and economic and work environments. Gaining a fine-grained understanding of the workplace is important not only because it explains why employees do what they do, but because it suggests ways that the workplace can be improved. The more we understand the subtleties of a workplace, the better equipped we are to design a work environment that encourages and facilitates learning, communication, and knowledge transfer.

Background

Over the past several decades, there have been enormous changes in the overall business environment. The number of manufacturing jobs has declined while the size and importance of the service sector has dramatically increased. Loyalty on the part of customers, employees, and employers has diminished. In addition, new computer and telecommunication technology has radically changed the shape of many industries. Not only has local competition intensified, but firms must now compete on a global scale. Because of all these changes, many managers view the future as increasingly unpredictable.

Firms and organizations—private and public alike—have become increasingly concerned with how they will adapt to this new and constantly changing business environment, and have begun to search for ways to reinvent themselves and gain a competitive advantage. Two strategies have become commonplace. One is to introduce or increase the use of information and communication technology in order to enhance productivity. The second is to emphasize learning, communication, and shared knowledge within the firm or organization, and to develop a work environment that is variously called a learning organization, occupational community, or community of practice.

The idea of community, which has long been associated with physical location and social groups (for example, small towns and neighborhoods), has migrated to the workplace and marketplace. The concept of communities of practice—a group that constantly shares knowledge and information—is based on the assumption that learning, whether it be formal or informal, is essential to the health and well-being of the organization. It also often assumes that information technology will act as the means to both store and share that knowledge and to support communication and collaboration within that specific work-based community.

Information technology (IT) is seen as key to reorganizing the workplace and coping with the changing business environment. The early emphasis of IT in the 1950s and 1960s was on introducing hardware and software to manage and manipulate data. More recently, however, communication technology has opened up new possibilities in the workplace by offering colleagues, who may or may not be located nearby, new ways to communicate synchronously and asynchronously.

Employee training is also seen as key to remaining competitive by ensuring that staff keep up with changes in their field of expertise. Learning in the workplace traditionally has focused on formal training and classroom-based learning, with U.S. companies spending billions of dollars annually on employee training. But recent research (EDC 1998) has found that up to 70 percent of the learning in the workplace actually takes place informally outside the classroom.

IT and training have long been considered tools for gaining competitive advantage, but traditionally they have been quite separate fields. Over the past few years, however, they have become deeply interconnected as communication technology has become pervasive in both the workplace and the home. Technology that was once used to simply manage data is now also used for sharing that data, for communicating and sharing knowledge among employees, and for distance education. As the line between IT and communication has blurred, so have the physical boundaries of the workplace; customers, workers, managers, and the head office may no longer be physically co-located, and the dissolution of these boundaries has created as many challenges as opportunities for firms and organizations.

The desire to use IT to enhance communication, learning, and sharing of knowledge is widely shared by many organizations, firms, and groups. Though the adoption and use of computer and communication technology offers the possibility of facilitating communication between employees, implementation has been challenging. Firms and organizations have struggled, faced with obstacles including competition between workgroups or employees, lack of incentives, inability of individuals or workgroups to articulate knowledge, and workers who are geographically remote or institutionally independent. It has not been easy.

Automobile manufacturers and their dealerships are good examples of the problems many firms and organizations face. A company's head office is centrally located, and its dealerships are widely distributed throughout the country and the world. Automobile companies have an additional unusual organizational feature—even though the manufacturer and the dealerships are highly interdependent, the dealership staff are not employees of the auto company; each dealership is independently owned and run. The head office can offer incentives and try to coax dealerships, but it ultimately has no direct management control. Not surprisingly, there can be tension in this relationship, because dealers often feel that the head office is overstepping its role and trying to micromanage their businesses. On the other hand, it is understandable why the manufacturers want and need the control—they depend on the dealerships to sell and service their products. Dealerships are the company's public face, and in a time when there is intense pressure to increase customer loyalty, manufacturers are very sensitive to how customers are treated.

The case of automobile dealerships is instructive for several reasons. First, their impact on the economy is significant: they generated $699 billion in sales and employed over 1.1 million people, with a payroll of $51 billion in 2005 (NADA 2006). In addition, the organizational model and relationship between dealers and the manufacturer is similar to a franchise relationship, in spite of common perception. In contrast to most franchises, which are understood to be owned and operated by individuals, the public generally views auto dealerships as simple extensions of the parent company and indistinguishable from the manufacturer. In truth, auto dealerships have much in common with franchise businesses, which can range from fast-food restaurants to hotel chains to personal services such as moving companies and dog grooming. They all have a similar structure and all struggle with similar issues, including enforcing control and standards, providing training, supporting management, and learning from and communicating with their franchisees (Bradach 1998).

The automobile industry has changed a great deal since the early 1990s. The design and manufacturing cycle has shortened and vehicles are much more complex, which means that service departments have had to cope with constant change and technological innovation. The quality of the vehicles has improved, and the differences between the makes are becoming smaller. However, competition among manufacturers and among dealerships is even more fierce. Profits for new car sales, the traditional source of revenue for the dealerships, are down, and attention has shifted from new vehicles sales to the service department. Customers are changing as well. They are less loyal to any particular brand; gone are the days when customers proudly referred to themselves as a "Chrysler man" or a "Ford family." Customers have become more knowledgeable and discriminating, and expect to be treated with respect. Customers are also much more willing to gain information about vehicles and the sales process from the Internet, with some even purchasing their new cars and trucks online, all of which has undermined the traditional role and power of the local dealer.

The Problem

The project of exploring automobile dealerships began when a major automobile manufacturer (referred to in this book as the GFC Motor Company) was looking for a solution to a problem. Like many other firms, GFC was concerned about the rapidly changing business environment and felt that increasing the flow of information between the dealerships and the head office would give it a competitive advantage. After all, the dealerships were on the "front lines" with the customers. Dealers knew a lot, and if that knowledge about vehicles and customers could make its way back to the Detroit head office more quickly and effectively, GFC would be better able to respond to problems, and ultimately to make better vehicles that customers would want to buy.

During the 1990s, the GFC Motor Company had made a great effort to deal with the changing business environment by introducing information technology and increasing training for dealership staff. It had already invested millions in a large private satellite system that linked several thousand GFC dealerships in the United States and Canada to the head office in Detroit, Michigan. The system was used primarily for distance education, broadcasting training programs to the dealerships throughout each workday, six days a week. Believing that keeping ahead of their competition required learning new ways of performing ordinary tasks and taking advantage of the knowledge that already existed within the firm and the dealerships, managers in Detroit proposed that the satellite system be expanded and used for two-way communication. Their aim was to use information and communication technology to encourage dealership employees to increase learning and sharing of information between Detroit and the dealerships, thus shaping their company into more of a learning organization. They also suggested that the new technology could improve communications with customers.

It sounded like a perfectly reasonable goal. The Detroit managers, however, perceived that there was a problem with the dealers and employees in the dealerships. Though there was no outright objection to or rejection of the idea, the dealership employees seemed to be, at best, lukewarm in their enthusiasm for information technology, learning, and sharing information with Detroit. GFC perceived the dealers' reaction as stonewalling and became increasingly frustrated with the dealerships and what it considered to be their uncooperative attitude. The head office very much wanted to know, "What's the matter with these guys?"

Wishing to increase the flow of information between the head office and the dealerships made a great deal of intuitive sense—it was hard to imagine any dealer, or manager of any firm for that matter, claiming that less communication and less learning could be advantageous to anyone. There already was a significant amount of information technology in place. If the employees and dealers were not apprehensive about becoming first-time computer users, what indeed was causing the problem?

Unfortunately the problem was not straightforward. It was not a simple case of dealership employees refusing to use information technology, because every dealership had and used computers. It was not that they refused to learn, because all employees already undertook some training each year. And it was not that dealership employees did not communicate with Detroit, because there was regular contact between the head office and the dealerships. The issue was one of underuse rather than non-use or non-adoption, and it was the lack of enthusiasm for increasing learning and communication using information technology that frustrated the managers in the GFC head office. Because they were in largely uncharted waters, it was unlikely that the answer was going to come from a preexisting set of traditional alternatives. In a case such as this, what they needed was to take a design-thinking approach.

Design

Though design is most often associated with buildings and artifacts, it can just as well relate to the creation of markets, institutions, policies, processes, programs, and services. Design thinking is not often discussed in management, but when it is, it tends to focus specifically on product development. Innovation, however, is an ongoing concern because continual innovation is assumed to be vital to a firm or industry. Innovation is the result of design thinking, but it too is more often used in the context of product development and less often in terms of technology, work organization, labor relations, or governance.

The definition of design is imprecise, but it is best defined as a way of thinking rather than a focus on its many possible products. Bryan Lawson (1997: 10) defines design as a "sophisticated mental process capable of manipulating many kinds of information, blending them all into a coherent set of ideas, and finally generating some realization of the ideas. It can take the form of a drawing, or a new timetable." Design is a skill that is learned, and is not, as is often assumed, synonymous with a stroke of genius. It is a prescriptive activity that deals not with questions of what is, and how, or why, but rather with *what might be.*

The idea of integrating design into management and management education is beginning to gain prominence. For example, Richard Boland and Fred Collopy argue in their book *Managing as Designing* (2004) that management education portrays the manager as choosing from an array of courses of action and assumes that coming up with alternatives is easy, but choosing is difficult. Rational decisions are made using a variety of tools such as economic analysis and risk analysis. In contrast, design assumes that coming up with good alternatives is difficult, but once a very good one is developed, the decision to go ahead with it is straightforward. The problem with the traditional rational decision approach is that it takes for granted that a set of good options is already available. Though this may be true in very stable and predictable environments, in a turbulent and unpredictable world, this assumption seems at best wishful thinking and at worse rather foolhardy. Design thinking is concerned with finding the best possible answer to complex problems given the goals and resources of the firm. It is about invention that includes questioning basic assumptions and reframing questions. It is not merely an artistic activity, but a humanistic and intellectual activity that focuses on the creation of practical and effective solutions that serve human beings (Buchanan 2004: 54). Design is a means of inquiry.

Regrettably, the design process is not a straightforward step-by-step procedure that can be followed irrespective of the situation. Instead, it is a rather mysterious affair with no simple formula or algorithm that can be applied to any given problem to derive the correct answer or solution. Many have tried modeling the process, but there has been little consensus, mainly because it can vary so much with the individual and situation.[1] But in spite of the range of models, there are some basic similarities: it is an iterative process that involves a "negotiation between problem and solution through the three activities of analysis, synthesis, and evaluation" (Lawson 1997: 47). One of the simplest models has the design process start with collecting information and understanding the context of the situation (Figure 1.1). Next is analysis, which explores relationships and patterns of the information gathered and identifies the problem or problems that need to be solved. But rather than leaving our understanding at analysis, the design process continues to move forward and respond to the situation by generating a set of proposals or solutions. And because it is an iterative process, the proposals are

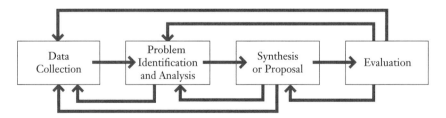

Figure 1.1. The design process
SOURCE: Data from Lawson 1997.

evaluated and reevaluated, often returning to earlier stages to gather more information, or to redefine the problem, until a solution appears that best answers or responds to the problem.

Framing the problem is key to the design process because how the problem is described will have direct consequences on the solution that is produced. A classic illustration of how problem-framing leads to a policy solution is Lloyd Etheredge's *The Case of the Unreturned Cafeteria Trays* (1976). The book examines the problem in a high school cafeteria of a minority of students not returning their cafeteria trays at the end of the lunch hour as instructed, leaving the cafeteria in a mess that had to be cleaned by the staff. Etheredge's book considers thirty ways of framing the problem, including ignorance of expectations, ignorance of consequences, too permissive an upbringing, inadequate identification with the school, and the Peter Pan syndrome. Each perspective suggests quite different solutions. For example, if it were a case of not knowing what was expected, the simple solution would be to inform the students about the expectation and need for them to return the trays. If it were a case of the students not understanding the consequences, then a tour of the messy cafeteria and an explanation by the cafeteria manager of the situation would likely suffice. Of course, if the problem stemmed from other more complex psychological issues, then the solution would be very different.

Not all problems are equal, however. Peter Rowe (1987: 39–41) describes three different types: well-defined, ill-defined, and wicked problems. Well-defined problems are those for which the ends or goals are prescribed and apparent and can be solved in a fairly straightforward manner. A structural engineer calculating the dimensions of a column or beam, for example, can apply specific formulae to estimate the appropriate size of the building member. Unfortunately most problems, whether they are social, architectural, or managerial, are more likely to be in the ill-defined or wicked categories. Ill-defined problems are those for which the ends and means of the solution are not known. Although the general direction may be clear, much effort and time is spent clarifying what is required. Wicked problems are problems without a definitive formulation. Questions are always being added, which leads to continual reformulation of the problem. Any time a solution is proposed, it can be developed further still.

The problem faced by the Detroit office is not unusual, especially in franchise-type organizations. GFC managers in Detroit assumed that they knew what the problem was—the dealership employees were being uncooperative—but were unsure what action they could take. The usual options of threatening termination or offering a financial bonus were difficult to do given that the dealership staff were not their employees. Their situation was typical—they thought they knew what the problem was, they saw the dealership staff as fairly homogeneous, and they had a handful of standard managerial remedial actions they would normally take if they could. In fact, what they actually had was an ill-defined and perhaps even "wicked" problem, which meant that the standard managerial responses to problematic employees would likely prove completely unsuccessful.

The purpose of applying design thinking to ill-defined or wicked problems is to define as clearly as possible what the problem is and to find reasonable solutions. The managers at the head office in Detroit assumed that there was something wrong with the dealership employees, as this would explain their lack of enthusiasm and cooperation. A design approach would question this assumption and begin to look for other explanations, which would point to more realistic and effective solutions. The goal was not just to understand why the dealership employees were behaving the way they were, but to also explore ways of creating an environment that would support learning and communication in the workplace.

I was intrigued with the problem that GFC was facing because what they hoped to accomplish, at least on the surface, made a great deal of sense. My past work had been in how local communities use IT to communicate, so I was also very interested in how information and communication technology could aid workplace organization.

The first step of trying to make sense of the situation began with data collection and gaining a deep understanding of the situation. This involved, in addition to shorter visits at several dealerships, spending many weeks over a period of months in a dealership that I will call Northeastern Motors. It was selected because it was considered to be a typical dealership by both GFC and the dealer. It was medium-sized, fairly busy, and average in almost every way. Both GFC and the dealer felt that the issues faced by Northeastern Motors were shared by almost every other dealership in the country. Perhaps the only slightly unusual aspect to Northeastern Motors was the employees' willingness to accept a stranger into their workplace and to talk candidly, though not publicly, about their work. This stage involved talking at great length with dealership staff about their jobs, observing them dealing with customers and going about their daily work, and participating in their training sessions.

It did not take long to see that GFC's framing of the problem was inadequate. The dealership employees were not Luddites, nor had they any great antipathy to learning or communication. Instead, their resistance, even aversion, to the urgings from Detroit to use information technology to learn and share more began to make perfect sense given their work history, culture, and environment. There were major problems and obstacles in the workplace, but there was certainly nothing wrong with the employees.

Understanding the reasons for the employees' reluctance to increase their use of IT for communication and sharing of information is important not only for the sake of GFC, but because the need to encourage learning, interdisciplinary collaborative work, and sharing of professional knowledge is a much wider issue. These are general problems faced by almost all organizations—private and public—and especially those with geographically distributed employees. The experience and lessons learned from GFC will be relevant to many. However, the point of this book is not that the solutions proposed for GFC should be blindly copied by other organizations. They should not be held up as "the answer," though they may be relevant for some firms. The purpose is to illustrate the process that organizations can undertake in order to create work environments that will encourage learning, communication, and sharing of information. That process involves close study and observation of the workplace, its history, and the employees who work in it, and then out of this rich understanding should come creative and appropriate solutions. Again, the point is not to copy GFC's solutions, but to encourage organizations to learn from and look closely at their own work communities and to find creative solutions based on their own unique experience.

As the following chapters will show, the managers in Detroit did not have a good understanding of the problem, and the handful of standard carrot-and-stick actions they could have taken would have been completely ineffective even if dealership staff were direct employees of the manufacturer. If they had approached the problem from a design perspective, not only would they have had a much clearer and accurate understanding of why dealership staff were so unenthusiastic about using technology for learning and communication, they would have been better equipped to take a number of steps that would have given them a higher probability of creating what they wanted—a learning organization.

Identifying Obstacles

To enable organizations and their employees to share information and learn from each other, communication is essential, but it is often assumed that a lack of flow of information between two parties is a problem of transmission, that is, having an inadequate "pipe" through which the information can flow. Indeed, in this particular case, that is an important issue, but it is not the only one. As George Huber (1996) points out, in order for information to flow, one needs to know who needs that information, and the information must be easy to transmit. But it is even more complicated because the sender must recognize that he or she has knowledge to transmit, and the receiver must be able to listen to and act upon that knowledge. The transmitted information or knowledge itself is also not neutral—whether it is threatening or affirming can prevent or encourage its flow. And not only are senders and receivers individuals with their own belief systems, but they work in environments with specific cultures and environments that may support or discourage the flow of the information.

Teasing apart the possible obstacles or barriers to learning and communication helps create a framework to more clearly investigate and understand the work environment. For any firm or organization looking to increase learning and communication, there are potentially six principal and interconnected obstacles that can block the flow of information or the sharing of knowledge between workgroups and colleagues: the physical environment, the medium, the content, the individual, the cultural and social environment, and the economic and work environment, all of which operate within a set of work practices, which operate within a specific industry or sector, each with its own unique history (Figure 1.2).

Physical environment. The physical environment in which the individual or groups work can have a significant influence on the learning and communication that takes place. For example, colleagues who work in separate parts of the building and who rarely have an opportunity to meet each other will have much less chance to communicate informally, and if their workspaces are noisy they may communicate even less.

Medium. The "pipe" through which information moves can block or impede the transmission if that pipe or medium is restricted, difficult to use, inaccessible, or simply does not exist. Though we usually think of the medium as the network through which the signal flows, it is not necessarily limited to the wires, cables, software, and hardware of computers or telecommunication systems. For example, the traditional office water cooler or the sales manager's desk has long provided the opportunity or medium for colleagues to meet and share information informally. Media can be electronic, physical, or administrative.

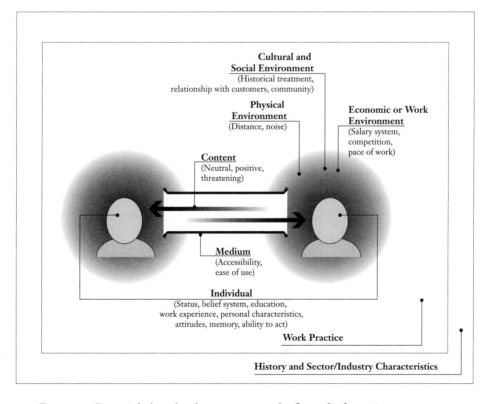

Figure 1.2. Potential obstacles that can prevent the flow of information

Content. The quality or type of information itself can impede flow. If information is perceived as negative or threatening, it can easily cause the listener to reject it. On the other hand, if the information is clearly useful and beneficial, the receiver will likely accept and make use of it.

Individual. Even in an environment that supports the sharing of knowledge, the receiver or sender of the information may hold a set of beliefs or memories that prevents him or her from either sending or receiving information. For example, individuals are unlikely to share knowledge if they believe that their information is not valuable ("Everyone already knows that") or if they have had a negative experience in the past ("No one was interested when I sent information last time, why should I bother now?"). The person receiving the information must also be able to "hear" the information and may reject it if he or she does not value the source ("What could a high-school-dropout mechanic ever tell me, a highly educated engineer?").

Cultural and social environment. The social or cultural relationship, history, and environment can also prevent the flow of information if some of the negative assumptions that individuals hold are shared more generally by the group. For example, in a hostile "us versus them" situation, there is unlikely to be an easy flow of two-way information. Or, if the group believes that sharing information will harm them in some way, there will be none.

Economic and work environment. The daily work routine and the economic environment are clearly some of the most significant factors that conspire against communicating and learning within an organization. Time pressure, competition, the salary system, and the single-minded focus on generating a profit each month all can hinder or severely limit communication and sharing of knowledge.

Work practices. The daily work is knitted together into a set of work practices. Individual work overlaps with colleagues' work and flows from department to department, as the staff person interacts with both customers and the manufacturer.

Industry or sector. Each learning experience or communication occurring in a firm or organization happens within the larger context of a certain sector or industry, which may influence how individuals and firms operate. And the sharing of information between firms will certainly be influenced by industry norms, assumptions, and levels of competition. In addition, each industry or sector has a historical dimension that may have an effect on learning and communication. Though establishing the effect of the past on current events may be difficult, it is generally assumed that the past can shape and inform contemporary events (Whipp and Clark 1986: 19), as well as industry standards, norms, and culture.

Because the auto manufacturer, the dealers, and the dealership employees face all six obstacles to some degree, we should not be surprised to learn that dealers and their employees may have been reluctant or even incapable of becoming the learning organization or community of practice that the head office desired. Clarifying the reasons for the dealership's lukewarm enthusiasm by identifying specific obstacles not only helps us understand and empathize with their predicament, but also points to concrete steps that could be taken to remove or reduce the barriers that hinder communication.

The following chapters use classic steps in the design process of *analysis, synthesis, and evaluation* to unravel the issues faced by GFC and the dealerships and to show the complexity of the workplace culture and environment. The analysis begins with an overview of the history and current state of the industry. It then describes typical work interactions in the sales and service departments with a pair of vignettes followed by descriptions of the work of service advisors, parts employees, technicians, and salespeople. Then, using the framework of potential challenges (and opportunities), the analysis considers the six categories: physical environment, medium, content, individual, cultural and social environment, and the economic and work environment. Finally, the synthesis and evaluation chapter proposes a number of possible solutions that GFC could adopt to increase learning and communication, ranging from the simple and easy to implement, to the much more difficult and challenging.

CHAPTER TWO

Automobile Dealerships—Past and Present

With a brand-new technology, high demand, public enthusiasm, and seem-ingly limitless opportunity, the early days of automobile manufacturing must have resembled in some ways the Internet start-up period of the late 1990s and early 2000s. But not everyone was convinced that the automobile had a bright future. To some it "appeared to be a fad, a rich man's toy, without long-term potential" (Critchlow 1996: 8). How wrong they were.

History of Automobile Dealerships

In its earliest days, automobile manufacturing was a business wide open to newcomers, and many eagerly took advantage of the opportunity. Although today's industry is dominated by a handful of companies, it was not always so—over five thousand automobile manufacturers have come and gone in the past century (Ketelle 1988). At the beginning of the twentieth century, the requirements to produce automobiles were rather modest and the assembly time was short. If you had even a small amount of money, the mechanical ability to put together a vehicle, and a place to do it, you could go into business. It was not necessary to make large capital investments in plant or equipment because an auto manufacturer at the time was essentially an assembler of components bought from outside firms (Rae 1965).

Once assembled, the finished vehicles were either sold directly from the factory or distributed to agents and dealers, and the money quickly flowed back to the manufacturers. "The demand for automobiles was so high that manufacturers were able to extract exorbitant concessions from distributors and dealers in exchange for exclusive territorial rights. Advance cash deposits of 20% were required on all orders, with full payment demanded immediately upon delivery through a sight draft attached to the bill of lading. And cars had to be accepted according to a prearranged schedule, regardless of current retail sales, thereby allowing the manufacturer to gear shipments to production" (Flink 1975: 43). "If parts were purchased with 30 to 90 days to pay, and if an advance deposit and the balance on delivery were demanded from the dealer, automobile manufacture became virtually self-financing" (Tedlow 1990: 116). It was a great time to be in the business. But unfortunately for the manufacturers, it did not last. By the 1920s, the technology and manufacturing process had become much more complex and required high levels of capital. The local metal shop was gradually forced out, and the industry became an oligarchy of large and powerful companies.

In the early 1900s, automobiles were sold by agents, and the earliest dealers were very often village harness makers, or the local farm implement dealer who sold automobiles as a sideline (Ketelle 1988).[1] Customers would place an order with the agent, who in turn would order the vehicle from the manufacturer, pick up the automobile at the train station, and deliver it to the customer. As business increased, agents found that they had to establish a place of business where they could display, sell, deliver, and service the vehicles. For some, the volume grew so large that they began to distribute their vehicles to other businessmen to sell (Marr 1985).

During the first half of the century, manufacturers also operated some factory-owned dealerships, selling directly to the customer—a system that continued in limited numbers until the late 1960s and early 1970s (Marr 1985). Factory stores always caused concern to the dealers because of the competition they created, but these stores played an important role in the early days because they also did final assembly. New cars shipped from the factory would be assembled at the factory store with factory-trained technicians. Dealership technicians would assist in the assembly (an early form of on-the-job-training) and then drive the finished vehicle to the dealership where it would be sold (Genat 1999: 20).[2]

Though initially cars were sold through agents, branch offices, traveling salesmen, or directly from the factory, by the 1920s, the model that we are most familiar with today—the independently owned franchised dealership—became the norm. The franchise restricted the dealer to selling a specified make or makes of new cars, the manufacturer fixed quotas of vehicles and demanded payment on delivery, and the dealer could lose the franchise at any time, depending on the whim of the manufacturer. The dealer had some territorial rights, but little effective protection against infringement (Rae 1984). The franchise agreement for the early dealers was a relatively straightforward two-page document. The dealer outlined the territory he was claiming and often attached a map as well. The requirements were also fairly simple: a facility from which to sell, proper signage, spare parts, and a mechanic to repair vehicles. Some franchises, such as Ford, also required the dealership to service all Ford cars, even those that had been purchased from other dealers (Genat 1999: 17–19). The franchises became more complex as time went on and as the relationship between manufacturer and dealer became more exclusive. Some of the new clauses in the 1926 General Motors franchise agreement were that the dealer would use an accounting system recommended by GM; the dealer would buy and use standard GM signs; the dealer would contribute $5 for every new car sold to an advertising fund controlled by the manufacturer; and a new "15 percent" clause gave the manufacturer the right to ship cars without an order any time the dealer had less than 15 percent of his yearly quota in stock (Spinella, Edwards, Mehlsak, and Tuck 1978: 56).

In economic terms, the franchise system was immensely advantageous to the manufacturers because it gave them "control without ownership" (Tedlow 1990: 145). But without the substantial investment on the part of the dealers, the early manufacturers simply would not have been able to survive. For example, in the 1920s, every Ford dealer had to invest approximately $5,000 in his dealership to get started. That sum, multiplied by the number of dealers in the country, equaled almost 15 percent of the value of the company, which was far more than Ford itself had invested in marketing (Tedlow 1990: 140). Dealers were and are an essential element to marketing automobiles, and most manufacturers have long recognized their importance. In fact, apparently one of the major reasons why Chrysler bought Dodge in 1926 was to obtain the Dodge network of dealers, which at the time was considered one of the best in the country (May 1989).

In spite of the fundamental importance of dealers, the relationship between the manufacturers and the dealers has often been an uneasy one, and dealers have long accused Detroit of abusing them and the franchise system. One of the more infamous past examples of how dealers have been treated badly is the Ford Motor Company's actions in the 1920s. When sales were dropping and the factory had a large inventory, "consignments of unordered cars were forced on over 6,300 Ford dealers, who had the choice of borrowing heavily from local banks to pay cash on delivery for them or forfeiting their Ford franchises. Henry Ford thus avoided going to the bankers himself and preserved his one-man rule and personal profits by arbitrarily unloading his financial problems onto the backs of thousands of hard-pressed small businessmen" (Flink 1975: 102; also see May 1989 and Rae 1984). And in 1926, even though production was cut, Ford increased the number of dealerships from 8,500 to 9,800 in the hope that increased competition would result in more aggressive sales. Instead, most dealerships lost money, some went bankrupt, and others switched to General Motors (Flink 1975: 106; Rae 1984: 57; May 1989: 311).[3]

Ford was not unique in its callous treatment of dealers, and other manufacturers were equally capable (and guilty) of being underhanded, unfair, and difficult employers and business partners. Another example, this time from the 1960s, concerns the Schwartz Dodge dealership in New Jersey, which Chrysler was accused of trying to destroy.[4] Manufacturers often claimed that they only put factory stores in a region as a last resort, for example, in areas where there was no other dealer, or where the dealer had abandoned the business. The Schwartz dealership apparently had been a very successful business, exceeding Chrysler's nationwide sales growth percentage for the previous five years. In 1966, Chrysler decided to expand Schwartz's territory to include the entire Newark metropolitan area with its several million people, and increase his minimum sales requirement accordingly, which he consequently failed to meet. Chrysler issued a notice of termination for the franchise. It eventually became known that Chrysler had planned to build a factory store in the area and wanted any competition eliminated, hence targeting the Schwartz dealership for removal. Schwartz went to court, and a judge issued an injunction to allow Schwartz to continue to sell Dodge cars (Ayres 1970: 122–124).

Still another example of how the manufacturers took advantage of the franchise system and infuriated dealers also occurred in the 1960s. Accessories, such as car radios, were an important source of income for dealers, who could make a profit on the part and collect a fee for the installation. This all changed when the manufacturers decided that they wanted that additional income. If a customer needed an air conditioner or car radio, instead of buying it from an independent company and having the dealer install it, the customer had to purchase the manufacturer's make, which was installed in the factory. The manufacturer took the profit and the installation fee, excluded the dealer from the transaction, and eliminated the customer's choice of brand (Ayres 1970: 125–126).

Although the relationship between the manufacturers and the stores has long been a source of tension, before 1920 the demand for new vehicles was so high that any friction was mostly ignored. In the late 1920s, however, when both the manufacturers and dealers were struggling to hold on to a declining market, the dealers became acutely and bitterly aware of the power the manufacturers had over their businesses. They complained about franchises that were issued without considering existing territorial rights, about unrealistic sales quotas, about being forced to accept unwanted cars, and about arbitrary cancellation of franchises (Rae 1965: 125). The National Automobile Dealers Association (NADA), which was founded in 1917 (Dicke 1992: 74), began to take on a role as a voice for the dealers.

By the 1950s, the dealers' grievances still had not been resolved, partly because dealers were reluctant to have government involved in their businesses in any way (even if it was in the form of legal protection), and partly because the dealers were not organized collectively. Some who were doing well did not want to complain and risk reprisals by the manufacturer, which could take the form of, for example, nondelivery of the best-selling models to their dealership, but delivery of an adequate supply to their competitors (Rae 1984). The Automobile Dealers' Day in Court Act, which was passed

in 1956, stopped some of the worst abuses, but the pressure that the manufacturers could exert on the dealers remained (May 1989: 312).

Though injustices had occurred, it was difficult for the government and
the public to be sympathetic to the dealers because the dealers themselves
had such a terrible reputation regarding their treatment of customers. Consequently there was more interest in protecting consumers from the dealers
than in protecting the dealers from the manufacturers.

In the 1950s there were an overwhelming number of complaints against
the "Big Three" (General Motors, Ford, and Chrysler) for their unethical
sales techniques. James Flink describes some of the worst: "The sales 'blitz'
was introduced in 1953, and high-pressure tactics came to include grillings
by teams of salesmen in special rooms equipped with bugging devices. Customers were subjected to the 'plain pack' (inflated charges for dealer preparation of the car); the 'top pack' (an inflated trade-in allowance added to the
price of the new car); the 'finance pack' (exorbitant rates of interest on in-
stallment sales, usually involving a kickback to the dealer from the finance
agency); the 'switch' (luring a customer into a salesroom with an advertised
bargain, then getting him to accept a worse deal on another car); the 'bush'
(hiking an initially quoted price during the course of the sale by upping the
figures on a conditional sales contract signed by the customer); and the 'high-
ball' (reneging on an initially high trade-in offer after the customer committed
himself to buying a new car). The customer might be induced to sign a conditional sales contract offering him a fantastic deal by a personable 'liner,'
who feigned sales inexperience; he would then be turned over to a tough-
talking 'turnover' man, who bullied him into accepting far worse terms, and
a 'stick man,' who cheated him on the financing. Salesmen often kept the customer from leaving the salesroom by 'unhorsing' him—taking his trade-in
out of sight to be 'appraised,' then refusing to bring back the car and/or return the keys. Few customers walked out of a salesroom without feeling that
they had been victimized, and many people still shop for a new car with trep-
idation" (Flink 1988: 281–282).

Automobile sales were extraordinarily high after the end of World War II,
but when sales eventually slowed neither the manufacturers nor the dealers
wanted to return to the days of more modest profits. The industry wanted to
sell seven million cars in a single year, two million more than in 1954, and a

half million more than the 1950 all-time record. "Automakers decided—either individually or collectively—on a way of accomplishing that goal. Quite simply, build them fast and send them to dealers. Any dealer who couldn't unload the vehicles on the public would lose his franchise or suddenly be faced with another same-make franchise within spitting distance" (Spinella et al. 1978: 70). In response, dealers had to find new ways of selling more cars. Hull Dobbs, a management firm specializing in sales techniques and hired by Ford dealers in the southeastern part of the United States, developed "The System," which involved luring the customer into the dealership by offering enormous discounts, free television sets, and mink stoles, and then not allowing that customer to leave without buying a car (Spinella et al. 1978: 70–73). "1955 would mark the end of any semblance of respect between customer and dealer. . . . Even now, America's auto dealers rue the day The System was hatched. Because it was this singular year and this one sales method which brought the wrath of government, consumerists and even the factories down on them. It marked the end of the automobile dealer as a merchant/citizen. From now on, the label merchant/con man was affixed—even for those undeserving of the title" (Spinella et al. 1978: 70).

Though the manufacturers claimed that their policies had nothing to do with these sales techniques, auto manufacturers must take at least partial responsibility for the unsavory reputation that auto dealerships acquired, as well as the unethical sales and shoddy service inflicted on the customer. Manufacturers forced dealers to accept too many cars and to keep large stocks of unwanted parts; they changed components frequently, which forced dealers to buy expensive new tools; they overcharged freight rates; they arbitrarily canceled franchises; and they located high-volume dealerships in areas where competition was already ruinous (Flink 1975: 192–193; Flink 1988: 282). Though manufacturers themselves did not sell the vehicles, they certainly created the conditions that resulted in high-pressure tactics and other unethical sales practices.

Consumer complaints grew to monumental proportions, and the government responded. Almost all of the worst aspects of "The System" were banned through legislation, including the Automobile Information Disclosure Act, which passed in 1958. The Act, sponsored by Senator Mike Monroney, a Democrat from Oklahoma, required every new car to have a price sticker (which is still called the "Monroney sticker") that lists all the items included in the vehicle and the manufacturer's suggested retail price, as well as the price of any optional equipment. Today this may seem a rather modest improvement, but at the time it was an enormous step toward consumer protection.

Automobile Dealerships Today

CHARACTERISTICS

Not only are automobile dealerships an important part of American culture, they play an important part in the nation's economy. In 2005 they employed over a million people, paid more than $50 billion in salaries, spent much of their $81.2 billion in expenditures locally,[5] and generated tax revenue on sales worth $699 billion.[6]

Though the automobile dealership as an institution continues to maintain its economic importance, the business and work life within the dealership has experienced major upheavals over the past twenty years. The small family-owned dealership is almost nonexistent, and the relationship between the dealerships and Detroit continues to be uneasy. Competition is much more intense, the balance of power between the service and sales departments has been upset, and most unsettling of all, the customer has changed. Adaptation has not been easy.

Though the total number of new-car dealerships has decreased by 3,000 between 1983 and 2003 to 21,725, the more dramatic change lies in the size of the dealerships (Figure 2.1). The number of small family-owned dealerships that sell fewer than 150 new cars per year has plunged from 8,600 in 1983 to 2,390 in 2003. Dealerships selling between 150 and 399 new vehicles per year have also decreased but not as sharply. In contrast, the number of very large dealerships has increased. Those selling 400–749 vehicles per year have increased from 4,100 in 1983 to 6,083 in 2003. And the largest new-car dealerships, selling more than 750 vehicles per year, have almost doubled from 3,500 to 6,952 over the past 20 years (NADA 2003).

Though there are fewer dealerships, the auto industry is still strong, with total dollar sales exceeding $699 billion in 2005. The market share of the "Big Three" manufacturers—DaimlerChrysler, Ford, and General Motors—continues to decline, from 73.38 percent in 1995 to 58.24 percent in 2005,

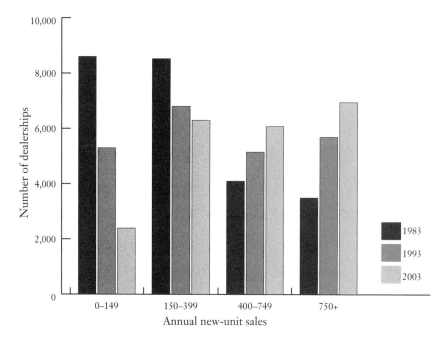

Figure 2.1. Number of dealerships, by volume of new-unit sales, 1983–2003
SOURCE: Data from NADA 2003.

with Toyota (13.34 percent), Honda (8.63 percent), Nissan (6.36 percent), Volkswagen (1.81 percent), and other imports (11.62 percent) making up the remainder.

RELATIONSHIP WITH MANUFACTURERS

One of the most distinguishing characteristics of an automobile dealership is its relationship with the manufacturer. The head office is commonly referred to as "the factory," dealerships are "the stores," and the relationship between them is often tense, even almost bitter. Naughton (1996) summarized the relationship between all automobile dealers and their manufacturers as "an uneasy standoff with Detroit."

Automobile dealerships are owned and operated by independent businesspeople who hire their own employees, none of whom are employees of the manufacturer. It is difficult to overemphasize the importance of this point, which is both independent and interdependent. The National Automobile Dealers Association, in *Dealership Organization and Management* (1973), describes the manufacturers as the heart of the industry and dealers as its lifeblood (12–13). It goes on to say, "The very first thing that should be understood is that the dealer is in almost every case an independent merchant, operating in his own facilities and with his own capital. The factory has no direct control over his day-to-day operation other than persuasion and, in the last analysis, the implied possible termination of the franchise agreement, which is something that is only used when all else fails" (188). It also notes that the essence of the franchising system is the dealer who has a substantial personal investment in the enterprise. This is important because it ensures the owner's close involvement in the business, which provides a reservoir of retail sales and management talent—none of which must be supplied by the manufacturer (13).

There are certain expectations in this partnership. The dealer expects the manufacturer to provide high-quality, reasonably priced, reliable cars that customers will want to buy. He[7] expects to receive vehicles when he needs them, detailed and current product information, competitive warranties, help with advertising, assistance in training his employees, and the assurance that he may keep his franchise as long as he performs up to standard. From the manufacturer's point of view, the dealer is expected to maximize sales, provide adequate service, stay in business, keep good records, and maintain the good name of the product (NADA 1973: 192–193).

The manufacturer often sees the dealers as difficult, and unwilling to change or innovate, so it tries to influence them through incentives, special programs, and sometimes not-so-subtle pressure. Not surprisingly, dealers can resent this intrusion into their businesses.

Dealers will often admit that the manufacturer's underlying ideas can be sensible and occasionally very good—it is the implementation that they usually disagree with. New programs are frequently considered to be overly complex, awkward, out of touch, theoretical, fussy, insensitive to geographic location, and unrealistic.[8] Dealers tend to believe that the corporate office simply does not understand what happens in the dealerships. And because most Detroit employees have never sold or serviced a car, dealers argue that they consequently should not have the right to tell dealerships how to run their businesses.

But there is more than a grain of truth in the Detroit managers' belief that dealers are unwilling to change or experiment. Many dealerships are wary of, if not resistant to, any idea that comes from the head office because they suspect that they will come out on the wrong end of any new arrangement. They feel that they have enough risk in their business without being the manufacturer's "guinea pigs." And because dealerships often find themselves in the position of having no choice but to accept the policies and programs from Detroit, they often do it halfheartedly, which in turn only further convinces the head office that the dealers just do not "get it" and need more pressure, motivation, and incentive programs.

COMPETITION

Not only do dealers face competition locally, they may soon be competing with their own manufacturers. Both General Motors and Ford are toying with the idea of creating regional superstores. The manufacturers would buy stakes in the dealerships; combine resources, inventories, and employees; and reduce the number of stores, thereby reducing competition between dealers. This new approach would feature no-haggling selling, salaried sales staff, and a Website that would allow customers to search the inventory from home. In addition, the centers would be supplemented by neighborhood service centers that would offer extended hours and no-appointment maintenance, warranty, and light repair work. The purpose of the experiment would be to create a nonpressure sales environment for the customer.[9]

The idea of the manufacturers being in competition with their dealers makes many dealers and salespeople deeply uneasy. Ferron and Kelderman (1984: 150) described the development of manufacturer stores as a "threatening wild card" to the franchise system. They feared the "prospect of a manufacturer, losing market share and with nowhere else to go, deciding that the only alternative is to abandon the dealers in order to lower the short-term costs of distribution dramatically. We don't know of any manufacturer in this frame of mind or financial condition, but we think the risk is sufficiently high to warrant attention to what has been referred to as a 'doom loop' judgment." It is also understandable why manufacturers would be interested in experimenting with new methods for selling their products. As Naughton (1996: 72) states, "Car makers would like dealers to improve the showroom experience. After all, they spend hundreds of millions of marketing dollars to turn their products into exalted objects of desire. And they spend hundreds of millions more to persuade consumers to step into the showroom—only to have them abused and alienated."

In principle, dealers certainly understand the need for change. It is clear that the world has changed and the old system of selling and servicing vehicles is becoming less viable, but what dealers fear is that the change will come at their expense.

SALES AND SERVICE

Major changes in roles and status within the dealership itself have also occurred, with the diminishing importance of the sales department and the increasing significance of the service and parts department. In terms of total dealership sales dollars, the new and used vehicle sales department is the overwhelming leader, making up 88 percent of total dealership sales dollars. But on the profit side, the picture is quite different.

The sales department was once the undisputed king, producing the majority of the average dealership's net profit. By the mid-1990s, the proportion of profits from new vehicle sales had tumbled until it was mainly a break-even operation, but by the late 1990s the situation had improved again. In 2005, the sale of new vehicles represented only 14.5 percent of the total operating profit, used-car sales made up 27 percent, and service and parts department profits accounted for 58.5 percent (NADA 2006). The service and parts department has become and continues to be an important player in the dealership hierarchy.

The sales volume of new vehicles has increased, and the average retail selling price of a new vehicle was $28,400 in 2005, up from $20,450 in 1995, but the sales department is still struggling. Profits are down, which translates into reduced income for those salespeople whose incomes are based on commission. Gross margins on the sale of new units continued to decline, from 10.18 percent in 1979 to 7 percent in 1992, dropping to 5.1 percent in 2005 (NADA 1992, 2006).

Though the service and parts departments are now an important part of the dealership, the transition has not been an easy one for them because they are in active competition with the independents—neighborhood mechanics as well as the franchised tune-up, brake, muffler, oil change, and transmission shops. Still, dealership service departments managed to reach sales of

$88.2 billion in 2005, only slightly down from the 2004 record, due in part to their effort to improve customer satisfaction and encourage customers to return to dealerships for vehicle maintenance and nonwarranty work. To help accomplish this, 66 percent of dealers offered evening or weekend hours in their service departments, with the average service department open fifty-four hours a week (NADA 2006).[10]

ORGANIZATION AND STRUCTURE OF A DEALERSHIP

Manufacturers and dealers are independent businesses, but are at the same time highly interdependent. To help with the coordination of their work, manufacturers will often have a regional field office layered between the corporate head office and the dealerships. Though the field office staff are employees of the manufacturer, they work as a liaison, representing the manufacturer to the dealership and promoting the dealers' voices at the corporate office. They also work with the dealers to help resolve customer complaints and misunderstandings, provide technical product information, and introduce any of the manufacturer's new programs or policies.

According to NADA, in 2005 the average franchised dealership had an annual payroll of $2,400,000 and employed fifty-three people with average weekly earnings of $870. Of the fifty-three employees in an average dealership, approximately eleven work in vehicle sales, twelve will be technicians, sixteen will be service and parts workers (other than technicians), and fourteen will be supervisors, general office workers, and others (NADA 2006). A busy medium-sized dealership would repair approximately 50 cars per day and sell 120 cars per month.

The typical dealership is hierarchical and is led by the dealer or general manager (Figure 2.2). Below the dealer are the managers of the four main departments: sales, office and finance, service, and parts. And below them are the salespeople, clerks, counterpeople, and technicians. Though a dealership officially has four main departments, in reality the dealership is split down the middle. On one side are the salespeople and office workers, and on the other is the service department, which includes customer service, parts, and the shop. Career paths are almost always vertical; few employees move horizontally, for example, from the service department to sales. There is also a sharp class division between the departments: sales and office staff are considered white collar while the service employees are usually blue collar.

Generally the relationship between service and sales is professional but distant, and contact between the two is minimal. Each, however, recognizes the need for the other and acknowledges their interdependency. As one service manager said, "The sales department is the engine that runs the dealership," meaning that unless the salesmen sell vehicles, the service department would have no work.

At the same time, friction is inevitable because the two units have very different cultures and two quite different relationships with the customer. Friction occurs when the service department does not satisfy a customer who then returns to the sales department to complain and asks for its intervention. Because the income of sales reps is related to the number of automobiles they sell and not the satisfaction of the customer after the sale, salespeople see any problem that flows over from the service department as financially unrewarding. For the salespeople, the less they see of recent customers, the better.

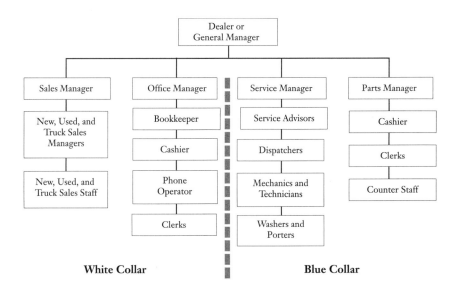

Figure 2.2. Organizational chart of a typical dealership
SOURCE: Sullivan 1962.

The departments have quite different cultures, types of employees, and work, and those differences are expressed (and reinforced) through clothing, behavior, and the physical environment. Salespeople are almost always dressed in suits—it is clear that they never have to get dirty—while the service advisors tend to be casually dressed and the technicians are in work clothes.

In addition to having different cultures and environments, the work practices of each of the departments vary significantly, with each having a very different relationship with customers, colleagues, and other dealerships.

CHAPTER THREE

Work Practice

Salespeople are quick to say that there is no typical sale because there is no typical individual or family, and in the service department every customer, every repair, and every day is a bit different from the next. But the following two vignettes, though not standard for every case, were compiled from observations of many different sales and transactions and are intended to give a sense of the process, the people, and the work involved when a customer brings in a vehicle for repair or arrives to purchase a vehicle at a fictional dealership called Northeastern Motors.

Vignette I: Service Department

Steve Harmon glances at his watch as he pulls into the entrance of the Northeastern Motors dealership and sees that it is a few minutes before 9:00. He is just in time for his appointment. As he begins to look for a parking space he sees a dealership employee waving him over. Bobby, who has his name and "Northeastern Motors" embroidered on his overalls, is the dealership greeter. He wishes Steve a good morning and asks about the traffic. As they are chatting, Bobby fills in a form on a clipboard, writing down the license plate number, the vehicle's make and color, and Steve's name. He also carefully notes if there are any scratches or dents on the car. There are none, but he is instructed to always check because some customers try to blame the dealership for preexisting damage. He opens the driver's door and bends down to copy the vehicle identification number. He then directs Steve to a door on a nearby building and asks him to go inside the service department, where they will take care of him. Leaving the keys and car with Bobby, Steve heads off to the customer entrance of the service department.

As he enters, the service counter is located just to his right with four people standing behind it. To the left is a fairly pleasant-looking waiting area. This is the first time he has been to this dealership, and he is pleased to notice a stack of current magazines, some comfortable furniture, and a television tuned to one of the morning talk shows. This is definitely an improvement from the last dealership he visited, which had never updated its old 1970s-looking waiting area with fake wood paneling, hard plastic chairs, old brochures, and dreary shag carpet. If he was going to wait here for his car to be repaired at Northeastern, at least he would be more comfortable.

Steve steps up to the service counter and introduces himself to a young man—the only person behind the service counter who is not with a customer. Tommy shakes hands with Steve and introduces himself as well. Tommy glances up at the whiteboard on the wall, as does Steve, who sees his name written next to the 9:00 A.M. slot and "Karen" printed in the service advisor column. Tommy explains that all customers are assigned to a specific service advisor so that they do not have to deal with a new person every time, and Karen will be with him in a moment. In the meantime, he would be happy to start the check-in process. At that moment, Bobby the greeter arrives with the keys to Steve's car as well as the paperwork, and hands them over to Tommy.

Tommy is pleased that Steve arrived on time. Not all customers do, and some arrive without making any appointment at all! In the 1970s and 1980s many dealerships did not take appointments, and customers could arrive at any time to have their vehicles serviced. That is no longer the case,[1] but not all customers are aware of, or remember, the new policy, and some still arrive unexpectedly, which inevitably leads to frustration and anger, especially if the customer cannot be rescheduled for several days or perhaps even weeks. The Northeastern Motors dealership tries to reinforce the importance of appointments by prominently displaying the whiteboard with the names of the customers, the service advisor, and the time of the day's appointment, usually spaced approximately fifteen minutes apart,[2] and it seems to work fairly well. Some dealerships actually prefer to use *drop off* or *write-up time* rather than the word *appointment*, because though they want the customer to bring in the car on time, they do not want the customer to assume that the technicians will start working on it immediately.

Tommy pulls up Steve's name and vehicle identification number on the in-house computer system to check if this is the first time that they have worked on this vehicle. Steve has recently moved to the area, so there is no record of previous work. Tommy types in Steve's contact information, and just then his colleague Karen finishes with her customer and says hello to Steve. Tommy explains to her that he has already put the telephone numbers and postal address in the system, but the description of Steve's problem with the car is all hers.

As he hands Steve over to Karen, Tommy wonders if it is too early to have another cup of coffee. Though it's only 9:00, he has already been at work for hours. As at most dealerships, the doors open at 7:00 A.M. and close at 6:00 P.M., or 9:00 P.M. at least one night a week. The service department is open six days a week, while the sales department stays open all seven. Tommy decides that perhaps the coffee can wait, but does take one of the fresh doughnuts that another service advisor brought in this morning.

Steve Harmon moves over to Karen's counter and begins to describe the noise that the window is making on the driver's side. She writes down the symptoms and description as he is talking, interrupting him from time to time to double-check the information—does it make the noise when the window goes up *and* down, or just going up? Mr. Harmon is good at clearly describing the problem. Not all customers are. What she does not know is that Steve had a very frustrating experience a couple of years ago with a service advisor at another dealership: he had taken in his wife's car because it was not starting reliably in the morning. The service advisor had grilled him about when exactly it happened, the weather conditions, the timing, the sound it made, and so on, and he realized that he could not answer them properly. He had to call his wife to find out more information, and he vowed to himself that he would spare himself future episodes with irritated service advisors by always arriving with a full, clear, and complete description of all the symptoms.

Karen has heard of this noise before from other customers, but because she knows that it is not the job of the service advisor to diagnose the problem, she conscientiously sticks to strictly describing the problem on the repair order. Before closing out, she checks to see if there are any recalls on Mr. Harmon's year and model of car. There are none. But if there had been, she would have printed them out and stapled them together with the repair order (RO). Because this repair is probably going to be fairly straightforward, she asks Steve if he would like to wait in the waiting area. She will call him the moment the repairs on the car are finished.[3] She tells him that he is welcome to have some coffee, and points to the door that leads to a hall where the vending machines are located. Steve picks up the morning newspaper and settles into one of the comfortable chairs.

Karen prints out the repair order and quickly walks it down the hall to Dennis, the dispatcher, whose job it is to take the repair orders that come from the service counter and distribute them to the technicians according to each technician's individual expertise, personality, and preferences. He is also required to schedule emergency or "special" jobs, such as work for a friend of the owner or for a client for whom they need to make a special effort. His job requires him to perform a delicate balancing act as he tries to juggle the pressure and needs of the customers, the dealership, and the technicians, but Dennis is good at it and he enjoys the challenge.

A skillful dispatcher is invaluable to the technicians in the shop because he or she mediates between them and the service advisors. In one dealership the software developers of the in-house computer system claimed that the dispatcher's job could be eliminated by developing a program that could distribute and schedule the work according to the technician's specialty and the estimated time to complete the job. The expert system failed because assigning these jobs to the technicians turned out to be much more complicated and subtle than the developers originally thought.[4]

Dennis takes a look at the repair order and realizes that it would be a very fast job for one of their technicians who has become the informal in-house expert at window assemblies, but unfortunately he is on vacation this week. It does not seem to be a very difficult repair, so he decides to assign it to Jim, who started working at the dealership a couple of months ago, and was just finishing up another job.

Jim arrives at Dennis's office to pick up the new repair order, and then logs into the in-house computer to start timing the job. If the repair were to be covered under the warranty, the manufacturer would insist that they keep track of the time spent doing the work, but at Northeastern Motors they always keep track of their time even if the GFC head office does not require it, because it helps them plan and manage their work better and makes for more accurate invoices.

As he is reading the description of the symptoms, one of the employees from the lot has driven Steve Harmon's car into Jim's service bay. From the description, Jim has a pretty good idea of what the problem is, but he checks the online system to see if there are any technical bulletins for that particular problem. Sure enough, there are. There have been repeated reports of a small part in the window mechanism failing on this particular make and model. It is a repair that is not difficult to do, so it should not take too long, assuming that the replacement part is in stock.

Jim gets into the driver's seat, starts the engine, and opens and closes the window several times to see if there are any additional sounds, vibrations, or clues that would tell him more about the problem, but the customer's description matches Jim's observations, and they both fit with the description on the technical bulletin. He will not need to take the car for a test ride, or use any of his diagnostic equipment for this job. Instead, he will be able to start the repair right away. On the computer near his service bay, Jim types in the part number for the assembly that will be replaced, which generates a parts order that is sent to the printer in the parts department. While he waits for the order to be filled, he starts to disassemble the door.

It only takes a few minutes to remove the door panel. As he walks over to the parts counter he greets another technician who is just leaving. Waiting for him on the counter is the window assembly he ordered. He calls a "thank you" to the guys back behind the counter, and as he heads back to his service bay, he thinks about how tough it must be for them to predict exactly what parts will be needed and in what quantity. But the manager of the parts department is both experienced and smart and seems to have a knack for knowing what will go wrong with customers' cars. Jim figures that it is a job that he is glad not to have. He prefers to install parts, not keep track of them.

Once back at his bay, he removes the old assembly and finds the failed plastic part that is making the squealing sound. He replaces it with the new one, reinstalls the door panels, and tests the window many times to make sure everything is working perfectly. Jim wishes all his work went as quickly and smoothly as this job. He types in a "story line" in the computer describing what he did and what parts were used, and then signs himself off the job, which stops the timer. The price of the part will be automatically charged to the RO by the parts department.[5]

Dennis, the dispatcher, looks up surprised to see Jim walk in and says, "Done already?" When Jim assures him that the work is finished, the part was in stock, and he is ready for a new job, Dennis jokes that at that speed he will take over as the department's window expert and so should be prepared to have more squealing windows sent his way.

Dennis has another RO ready, and while Jim is reading the new one, Dennis walks Steve Harmon's RO back to Karen. She is not there, so he leaves it on the counter and returns to his office.

Karen returns moments later—she had just run down to talk with the parts manager about a cab liner that a customer had ordered earlier in the week. When she sees the RO for Steve Harmon's car she is momentarily taken aback, thinking that the RO had been returned by mistake, but quickly sees that the repair has been done and all is well. She looks over at Steve, who is in the waiting area and seems to be engrossed in an interview on the television. She calls his name and tells him that his vehicle is ready to go. He takes a last sip of coffee and returns to the counter, where Karen prints out the repair order and invoice, hands them to him, and directs him to the cashier's office down another hall where he will pay.

As soon as Jim the technician finished the squealing window job and the RO worked its way back to the dispatcher's office and service counter, a washer or porter had taken Steve Harmon's car, washed it, parked it in the lot, and returned the keys to Karen at the service counter. The keys are waiting for Steve when he gets back from the cashier's office. Karen quickly reviews Steve's paperwork from the cashier to verify that everything has been paid for, and puts the keys in his hands. He thanks her for her help, and Karen says that other than routine maintenance, she expects and hopes that he will not need to be back to see them for a very long time.

As Karen waves goodbye, she thinks about how well that repair went. Not every job is as successful. Between 5 and 7 percent (and often more) of the vehicles that pass through the service department are returned because the original problem was not fixed. Not correcting the problem the first time turns out to be an even bigger problem than simply having to repeat the work, because GFC discovered that dissatisfied customers often did not complain directly to the dealership—if they did, the dealership would have had the opportunity to correct the situation. Instead, dissatisfied customers simply never returned. As a result, a new policy had been introduced. Service advisors now had to call customers two to three days after servicing to verify that they were satisfied with the work done. Karen makes a note to call Steve in a couple of days to make sure that all is well and the screech in the window has not returned. She is quite sure that the repair solved the problem, but she knows that Steve Harmon will appreciate the gesture, and hopefully he will recommend the dealership to family or friends.

Vignette II: Sales Department

A couple and their two young children enter the showroom on a weekday afternoon and walk toward the six shiny new cars in the center of the room. There are seven salespeople in the dealership that afternoon, but most are either with clients or busy working on paperwork. Bob, a salesman with ten years experience at Northeastern Motors, has finished his follow-up calls for the day and is pleased to see the family walk in. He claims that his intuition is usually accurate, and to him these customers look like serious buyers.[6]

He approaches them and *greets them* warmly—the first step in the sales process—taking care to look each of them, including each child, in the eye while introducing himself and shaking hands with the adults. Bob makes a comment about the threatening clouds gathering on the horizon, and they discuss the likelihood of snow and the disruption of their weekend travel plans. He then asks them how he can be of help.

The couple says that they now have a GFC sedan but are looking for a second car and are interested in a sports utility vehicle. Bob is now in the second step of the sales process—*gathering information.* He probes, asking about when the car will be used, by whom, and for what purpose. Bob and the other salespeople at Northeastern Motors believe that matching the right car with the needs of the customer is a priority. They believe that if the customers get what they need and want, then they are likely to return again in the future. (The philosophy seems to work because a large percentage of their business is made up of repeat customers.) The couple explain that they have a cabin in New Hampshire that they like to visit on weekends, so they are looking for a fairly good-sized vehicle with four-wheel drive that can hold all of them and their gear comfortably. During their conversation, Bob finds out that the couple, like himself, enjoys fishing on the lakes near their cabin, and he makes a mental note to record this in his database. He finds that the more he knows about his customers and the more they have in common, the better, because good rapport helps Bob sell cars.

After listening carefully and repeating what he has heard to ensure that he understands what they are looking for, he says that he has a couple of *vehicles that he would like to show them*—the third step in the sales process. He asks how much they are thinking of spending in monthly payments, but the couple are savvy buyers and say that they would like to see the vehicles first and talk money later.

Bob shows them the Adventurer—one of Northeastern's most popular models—and discusses possible options. He invites the two children, who are becoming visibly bored, to hop in the car to see what they think. The parents look pleased at his thoughtfulness. On his part, Bob is relieved that this couple seems to be straightforward and easy to deal with. He has a lot of customers who are suspicious and defensive and assume that Bob is the stereotypical fast-talking, cheating car salesman. This frustrates him because he is conscientious and ethical, and Northeastern Motors insists that their salespeople treat customers honestly and fairly—a dishonest salesperson would simply never be permitted to work there. But he also acknowledges that not all dealerships follow that philosophy, and he understands that customers are usually suspicious because they have had bad experiences in the past.

The couple has obviously done their homework and seems to be quite knowledgeable about the vehicle. When he mentions this, they say that yes, they had done some background research on the Internet. Bob, unlike some salespeople who resent customers who know a lot about the product—sometimes more than the salesperson—accepts this with equanimity. His attitude is that if customers have a very clear idea of what they want, then it simply makes his job easier. He does worry though about the quality and accuracy of information that customers get on the Internet, but it does not seem to be an issue with this couple. Bob also keeps up with similar products made by other manufacturers, so he is able to knowledgeably discuss the advantages of the Adventurer over the competitors' products. The couple seems very interested in what they are seeing, but Bob also wants them to take a look at the Safari—a higher-end SUV that is on the floor. Indeed, they are very impressed with it and remark how much they like it, but after a quick look at the manufacturer's suggested retail price (MSRP) on the window sticker, they sigh and say that as much as they like it, it is way out of their price range. Bob jokingly says that in that case, he will put one away for them— they can buy it when they are ready for their next car—and they all laugh.

Bob suggests that they go back to his desk to talk for the fourth and probably most important step—*price negotiations.* On the way back he picks up some of the promotional balloons in the showroom to give to the two children to play with while their parents talk.

The desk that Bob sits at is not actually his—he shares it with another salesperson who works a different shift—but he always puts out his name plate and a picture of his family on his desk. Displaying family photos is a common and old sales technique used to convince customers that the salesman is a solid, trustworthy, family man—and Bob uses it not only because it works but because it provides another potential topic of conversation with customers. He first writes down their names and contact information. This is important because if the customer decides to leave the showroom without buying a vehicle (which is typical), he will be able to call them back to see how their search is going and ask if there is anything he can do for them. He tries once again to find out how much the couple is willing to pay, but again they say that they would like to first hear an offer from him. Because the customers are experienced buyers and have obviously done research on the vehicles, he (correctly) assumes that they have done the same research on the buying process that is now readily available on the Internet. Because they probably already know what the consumer guides recommend, he does not begin with the MSRP, but a number somewhat lower. That is not acceptable, and the couple counteroffer with an amount 1 percent over dealer invoice. That amount is unsatisfactory for Bob, but he is relieved that at least they are not negotiating the holdback—the 3 percent under invoice that some customers insist on.[7] They discuss the options package once again, and he says that he can only give it to them at the price mentioned if they are willing to give up some of the options they wanted. They discuss whether they really need the four-door, and agree that they do. Bob makes a counteroffer, 6 percent over invoice. That is a little higher than they wanted to pay, so after more discussion, they decide to leave off a couple of options, and agree on a price that is 4 percent over invoice. It is not a great price for either party in Bob's opinion, but it is certainly reasonable. The price means that the dealership will earn a profit of $869, of which he will get 25 percent, or $217.

Bob records the price that they have agreed to and stands up to say that he just has to get it approved by the sales manager. The couple looks slightly surprised, but he explains that all salespeople must have all sales offers approved by the manager. Pricing can be complicated, and because the document is a binding legal document, the dealership must be sure that they can uphold their end of the bargain. Because Bob is experienced and knowledgeable, the couple is not trading in a car, and the vehicle is available on the lot, the sale is straightforward, and the sales manager signs it readily. Bob is soon back at his desk with the document in hand. The couple accepts it, but say that they would still like to think about it and maybe look around a bit more. Bob was hoping for a deal today, but he does not show his disappointment. At this point in the sale he could put enormous pressure on the couple to sign—an approach called "buy or die"—but he prefers, as do others at Northeastern, to let the customer walk out the door. If they were treated well and were given a fair price, then most likely the customer will return. In this case, Bob is almost positive that he has a sale. He gives them his card, invites them to call him at any time, and says that he hopes to hear from them soon.

The next morning, Bob calls the couple to ask if they have been able to give it any more thought or if there is anything that he can help them with. They say that they like the vehicle a lot, and the price was slightly higher than they had wanted to pay, but have decided that they can live with it. They also admitted that they had gone to other dealerships, but were not happy with how they were treated, so yes, they are going to buy the vehicle, and they want to know how soon they could get it. Because the vehicle is in the lot, Bob says he will have it cleaned and prepared for them and they can pick it up that afternoon.

Bob is pleased that the couple decided so quickly because it is not unusual for weeks to go by before customers make a final decision. This sale was easy in comparison with others and made up for the slightly lower price that he earned on the vehicle.

That afternoon, the couple comes in again with their two children, who volunteer the information to anyone within earshot that they are there to buy a blue car. They are greeted by Bob, who is expecting them, and the two adults go into the F & I (finance and insurance) office with the dealership's business manager for the fifth step—*closing the deal* and final signing of papers. Here the manager takes advantage of the last opportunity to sell the customer additional products and offers them services such as extended warranties, additional rust-proofing, insurance, financing, and security systems. The couple already has insurance and financing arranged, so they decline the offers. They do, however, decide to take the extended warranty, which is added to their invoice.

Once all the papers are signed, the couple returns to Bob's desk, where he gives them a rundown on the vehicle's maintenance schedule, tire rotation and pressure, driving tips, and warranty information. He acknowledges that this is a lot of information to absorb but that it is also written in the manuals that he has for them. He makes a point of explaining that the keys have a small computer chip in them so they cannot be copied at a normal key shop. If they lose them, or want copies, it will cost $50. The couple joke that they will try not to lose their keys at that price. Bob then walks them out to the service area, where he introduces them to Karen, one of the service advisors, as well as Bob, the service manager, who happens to be standing at the front counter. He has them make an appointment with Karen to return in ninety days for a filter change. The idea behind introducing them to the service side of the dealership is that they want the couple to return to them for all repairs and maintenance in the future rather than go to the corner garage.

The last stop is the vehicle out in the lot. Bob wants to make sure that they understand how a special feature works on the four-wheel drive because they will probably be using it that weekend on their drive up to New Hampshire. He shakes hands with the family, tells them it was a pleasure to meet them, and that he hopes to see them again when they are ready for the Safari. He says that if there's anything he can do for them in the future to not hesitate to call, and they assure him that they will. Bob is confident that if the vehicle lives up to their expectations and if servicing goes smoothly over the next few years, he will have a repeat customer with this family, and if he is lucky, he may even gain new customers through their friends and families.

The Work of Dealership Employees

Even though the number of employees in the average dealership is not large, the work of each employee group within the dealership—service advisors, parts employees, technicians, and salespeople—differs significantly. The following is an overview or synopsis of each group's role within the workplace.

SERVICE ADVISORS

The role of the service advisor is essentially one of conduit or mediator between technicians and customers. At a small neighborhood garage the technician would probably talk directly to the customer, but at most dealerships the advisor draws out information about the vehicle's problem from the customer, passes it along to the technician, and, when the diagnosis and/or repair is done, passes the information from the shop floor back to the customer.

The job of a service advisor is to "show a happy face and get the maximum amount of information from the customer" as one service advisor described it, but showing that happy face is not always easy because of the tension created by being caught between the technicians and the customer. Customers are usually unhappy about being in the service department because it means that something is wrong with their vehicle. In addition, they feel vulnerable and assume that they will not be treated fairly by the dealership staff. Paul Marr describes this often unhappy atmosphere thus: "The attitude and nature of the typical customer is much different than is found in many other service businesses. He/she has not made an arbitrary decision that this is a service they would like to purchase. Rather, it is something that the customer is most often forced to do because of a failure of the product; there is no pleasure or enjoyment involved. People are not generally happy to need vehicle service—people do not want to buy vehicle service. Obviously the customer is often upset and angry, resulting in a negative server/customer environment. This can make the service challenge for the dealership employees a difficult one" (Marr 1985: 77).

Service advisors are also frequently the bearers of bad news. They have to cancel appointments, justify why the customer's bill is so large, explain why the customer's car is not ready at the promised time, and describe the often obscure details of the customer's warranty contract and why it may not cover the cost of the repairs. In response to the bad news, customers tend to direct their anger and frustration toward the service advisor. As NADA (1973: 122) delicately puts it, "Psychological situations may arise such as the case of the customer having a real or fancied complaint," and they recommend when this happens that the service advisor try to counsel and placate the customer, and if this proves unsuccessful to bring in the service manager.

Service advisors also walk a tightrope between the dealership management and customers. Service advisors actually have quite a bit of decision-making power and flexibility, but this can also get them into trouble. If they are too lenient with the customer, the dealership management can accuse them of being too "soft" and reducing the department's monthly profits. But if they are too strict, management can still criticize them for provoking the customers' anger by not being flexible enough.

The service advisor's job is one of the most difficult in the dealership simply because so much can go wrong. They can underestimate the time needed for repairs and overbook the day's schedule, which frustrates the technicians and dispatchers and obviously annoys the customers when they do not get their vehicle back on time. Or if the service advisors overestimate the time and there is not enough work in the shop, they will be in trouble with both the technicians and management.

One of service advisors' greatest challenges is to get accurate and detailed information from the customer. Customers can be vague about a problem, they can have difficulty describing the symptoms, they may conceal information that makes them look foolish and so more vulnerable, or they may just agree with anything the advisor says. To help rectify this, some of the manufacturers, including GFC, have produced aids to help get more accurate information from the customer. For example, they may have a symptom code worksheet that helps the customer describe the vehicle's problem, which includes a list of the sounds that the customer might hear (for example, boom, buzz, chatter, chirp, chuckle, click, clunk, grind, groan, growl, hiss, hum, knock, ping, rattle, roar, rumble, squeak, squeal, tap, whine, whir, and whistle). If driveability is a problem, there are lists of symptoms (hard start, no start, runs rough, hesitates, surges, backfires, and so on), as well as detailed questions about where and when noise, vibration, and driveability issues are occurring. Not all advisors use these aids, however, and they are not clear themselves about why they choose not to use them. It could be a sense of pride ("real advisors don't use aids") or it could be that these aids lengthen a difficult and frustrating conversation that the advisor would simply prefer to end as quickly as possible.

Even though customers can be vague about the description of their vehicle's problem when they arrive, they can be very demanding about the details after the repair has been done. Advisors often resent this, and some consider it a form of harassment, but the customer's demand for information is probably much more benign than the advisor realizes. The customers may simply be trying to educate themselves and exercise some control over the situation—they do not want to look quite as inadequate as they feel, and they certainly do not trust the dealership enough to blindly accept any explanation that the service advisor gives them. Customers may also demand information as a way of assessing whether they have been charged fairly.

Another issue that both service advisors and customers face is in the gray area of defining what constitutes a "problem." An example of an ambiguous problem is a customer who comes in complaining about a hole in the carpet on the driver's side of her vehicle that is less than a year old. From the service department's perspective, the carpet has worn through because there is a weld joint where the customer rests her foot, she is tall, she wears leather heels, and the carpet quality is not the best. The hole will occur when those conditions exist, and therefore it is not a problem because it is not a puzzle or a surprise. In this case the dealership is unwilling to accept blame or responsibility for something that they consider to be "normal," and if anything, a cosmetic rather than a safety issue. From the customer's perspective, however, being tall and wearing street shoes is not reckless, unreasonable, or wrong. The vehicle she bought was expensive, and the carpet seemed to be of a reasonable quality. One can be absolutely sure that a salesman never warned her that her height or footwear could be a liability, or that the carpeting was not the best quality. For the customer, wearing a hole in the carpet within a year was not normal, reasonable, or acceptable—it was a problem.[8]

PARTS EMPLOYEES

The work of the parts department revolves around ensuring that the technicians have the parts they need to repair the vehicles brought in to the service department. Technicians are the parts department's primary customers, while retail and wholesale customers, though important, are often considered in many dealerships to be less of a priority.

The main challenge for parts employees is to understand just what it is that the technician or the customer is requesting. Communicating with retail customers can be especially exasperating if they arrive without crucial vehicle information such as the year, type of transmission, or type of engine. Wholesale customers, on the other hand, tend to be easier to work with because they are usually technically knowledgeable. But even with technical knowledge and complete vehicle information, identifying the right part is not easy and gets more difficult every year because of the increasing complexity of cars and number of models—the "ever expanding universe of parts," as one manager described it.[9]

Ordering and maintaining the correct balance of stock is a complicated system of obsolescence programs, return percentages, and calculations for special types of orders. Orders are sent in weekly, and the parts arrive within a couple of days. It would be ideal if any part a technician ever needed was on the shelf, but keeping a large and varied stock is extremely expensive and takes up an excessive amount of floor space. Parts managers estimate the quantities they will likely need, keeping in mind that they are penalized by the manufacturer if the parts sit on the shelf longer than six months. It is difficult to anticipate just the right number and the right type of parts, because it is impossible to know with certainty what type of repair work will come into the shop at any given time. Given these circumstances, running a smoothly functioning parts department takes a blend of experience, wise judgment, and a dose of good luck.

TECHNICIANS

The work of a technician consists of picking up a repair order from the dispatcher for the next vehicle he[10] will work on, carefully reading the symptoms and description of the problem, taking it for a test drive if necessary, or performing a variety of diagnostic tests. Depending on the results of the tests, the technician will research technical bulletins issued on the problem, and then make the adjustments or repairs.[11] If new parts are required, he will send the request to the parts counter and a few minutes later walk over to pick them up. The technician will then replace the parts, ensure by using test equipment or taking the car for a test drive that the problem has been solved, log off the job on the computer, and then contact the dispatcher for the next job (Figure 3.1). In the meantime, a porter or assistant will remove the vehicle from the service bay and park it in the lot.

Technicians have a uniquely ambiguous role in the dealership. They are the ones who do the "dirty work" and have a job that is clearly blue collar. Yet their work is highly skilled and they are paid quite well—often substantially more than some of the white-collar workers in the dealership. Though they may not have high-status "clean" jobs, good technicians are prized by customers, the service department, and the dealership.

The transition of the technician's perceived role from a lower to higher status is illustrated in the words used to describe the job. Ray Sullivan (1962)

Figure 3.1. Computers are used extensively in the technician's service bay

discussed the use of the words *grease monkeys* and *mechanics* and how vehicle manufacturers and dealerships worried that the dismissive names would discourage young men from taking these jobs. Consequently, the Ford Motor Company, for example, has referred to service department personnel as "Ford Service Technicians" since 1959. "The Ford Div. recognizes the value of these skilled men who are so dedicated to their profession that they take time for study and work to improve their experience and ability. Therefore, we feel that the time has come to set up a new term to describe the skilled men who work exclusively on the maintenance, repair and adjustment of our complicated modern automotive vehicles" (Sullivan 1962: 134).

SALESPEOPLE

Dealership salespeople have a unique and unenviable relationship with their customers because, deserved or not, the view of car salesmen as unsavory and untrustworthy characters is ever present. Of course, the reputation is not groundless, stemming as it does from customers' experiences over the past seventy years and the structure of the sales process itself. No matter how much the manufacturers try put a more positive spin on their new approach to sales (making it a friendlier and more pleasant experience), auto sales is a zero-sum game in which the more the customer pays, the more the salesperson makes.

Because the goal of the salesperson is to get the customer to pay the highest possible price, automobile sales in the past have often focused not on matching the automobile to the needs of the consumer but on a process of mildly "tricking" the customer or winning a game. A guide from the early 1960s, *The Automobile Dealer and His Employees: A Management Guide to Assist New Car and New Truck Dealers in Building and Retaining an Efficient and Progressive Organization* (Sullivan 1962: 99) listed the techniques that salesmen should use to make a sale. None were illegal or misleading, but all were intended to "reduce tension and relax the buyer's defenses." Some of these included the friendly appeal ("Now, Mr. Smith, I'll tell you what we can do for you."), suggestive appeal ("Rather than avoid a slow-down, give the customer time to back out, go right from your sales presentation into a suggestion that 'we get the car out to you next Wednesday.'"), premium close

("Hold back an extra—a special point that you know will be enticing—and spring it after the entire presentation is over."), and close on a minor point ("A technique which often works is to ask the customer, 'What color do you prefer'? When he answers 'black', assure him that he will get a black car as soon as it is possible to get ready" (Sullivan 1962: 98–99).

Today no dealer or manufacturer would ever publicly recommend using these kinds of "techniques." In fact, most manufacturers go out of their way to urge salespeople to look at sales as a win-win process. But in spite of the good sense of this approach, the system remains—salespeople are rewarded for getting customers to pay the highest price possible. Consequently, it should be no surprise that customers feel resentful and vulnerable—they are not expert at the car-buying game, they operate with minimal information, and a lot of their hard-earned money, to say nothing of their pride, is at stake.

Without doubt, buying a vehicle has to be one of the most confusing and opaque processes that a consumer has to go through. After all, as one salesperson laughingly asked, where else do you go to buy something but no one tells you exactly what the price is? This vulnerability, suspicion, and lack of accurate information have led to a surge of consumer information in print and online. *Consumer Reports*, which has long published print information on purchasing a vehicle, now also publishes online, as do a number of other groups and organizations.[12] Not surprisingly, salespeople are not very enthused about customers arming themselves against potentially unscrupulous dealers by becoming more informed. "A little knowledge is a dangerous thing," as one salesperson remarked. And of course they are not very happy with the sites that reinforce the stereotype of the sleazy salesman. One incensed salesman declared that a Website he had seen resembled a "terrorist handbook" because it described how customers could fight car salespeople with the same rudeness, disrespect, underhandedness, and deception that they could probably expect to receive.

Salespeople often see themselves as the victims of a difficult and unreasonable public. Honest salespeople are forever trying to live down their inherited reputation of being untrustworthy, and complain that they "are always seen as the bad guys." They complain that people are "rough," critical, and difficult, and do not want to pay a reasonable price. They see themselves as businesspeople who have to make a profit to stay in business, and they become exasperated with customers who have read everything there is on "beating the salesman" and expect dealers to sell them a vehicle at invoice, or sometimes even below. Wealthy customers cause the most frustration because of their tendency to want to "nickel and dime" the salesperson until they get the lowest possible price.

CHAPTER FOUR

Obstacles to Learning and Communication

As discussed earlier, the transfer of information is much more than having a pipe through which it can flow. The physical environment; medium; content; individual, cultural, and social environments; and economic and work environments will all influence communication and learning in the workplace. And as we will see, these potential obstacles will have a different impact on each of the dealership workgroups.

The Physical Environment

The earliest automobile dealerships commonly were located in downtown areas, often in converted sheds or storefronts. In the 1920s, purpose-built dealerships gradually began to appear, and by the 1940s manufacturers were publishing property and facilities planning guides (Genat 1999: 43). By the

1970s, dealerships were moving out to the suburbs, where the price of land was lower and where dealers could build vast purpose-built facilities.[1]

The interiors of the dealerships have changed as well. The original sheds were gradually transformed into the opulent and luxurious showrooms of the 1930s and 1940s. Images from the period exude elegance, with new cars displayed on individual Persian rugs, under chandeliers, and surrounded by leather chairs, ornate woodwork, potted palms, and fresh flowers. After World War II the showrooms' appearance became "formal and cold" (Spinella, Edwards, Mehlsak, and Tuck 1978: 82), and from the 1960s to 1990s, showrooms could charitably be described as "minimalist." Some dealers during this period made an attempt to make their showrooms somewhat more appealing, but for most every expense was spared. By 2000, dealers who were expanding or renovating were making a much greater effort (and investment) in making their facilities more attractive, appealing, and comfortable for customers, with some even including child-care facilities and espresso bars.

The physical form of the typical dealership's floor plan accurately reflects the social relationships between employees and the customer, as well as between the sales and service departments (Figure 4.1). Genat (1999) notes that when new dealership facilities are planned today, approximately 73 percent of the total floor area is allocated to the service department and 10 percent to the parts department. The remainder is for the sales department and administration.

In the service department, customers have access to the service advisors, the cashier, and a counter in the parts department. In terms of physical movement, the service advisors have the widest travel range in the dealership, and though they are usually in their place at the service counter, they will also walk back into the service bays and parts department to talk with technicians and staff. Technicians sometimes walk up to the service counter, and they regularly go the parts counter, but they do not enter the room where the parts are stored. Parts staff stay within their department, serving retail customers and technicians from behind the counter. Customers enter either the sales or the service department; passing between the two departments is rare.[2]

The diagrammatic plan also indicates the areas of the dealership that are considered "dirty," an issue that comes up with some regularity when describing both the work of the service department employees and the design of the physical spaces within the dealership. Both the 1957 and 2004–2005

Occupational Outlook published by the U.S. Department of Labor, Bureau of Statistics, emphasize the dirty and physical aspect of work in the service department. "In most jobs, the mechanic handles greasy tools and parts, and it is often necessary for him to stand or lie in awkward or cramped positions for extended periods of time" (Stambler 1957: 24). "Although they fix some problems with simple computerized adjustments, technicians frequently work with dirty and greasy parts, and in awkward positions. They often lift heavy parts and tools. Minor cuts, burns, and bruises are common. . . . " (Bureau of Labor Statistics 2004).[3]

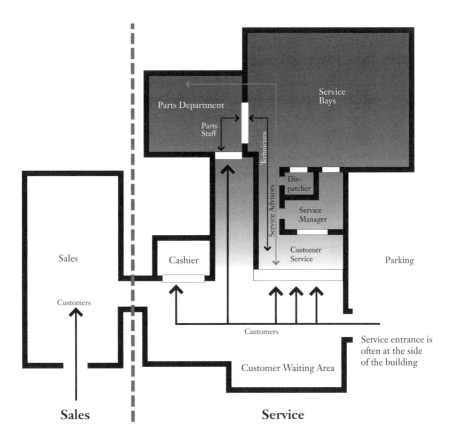

Figure 4.1. The physical layout of a dealership

NOTE: This floor plan is diagrammatic only and is not to scale. The gray in the diagram indicates the areas that are considered "dirty."

The issue of cleanliness and ambiance is also considered in the design of automobile dealerships. The author of a 1956 thesis explained that "the types of spaces are easily divisible in two distinct groups, and are expressed by two separate buildings. First is the clean and quiet atmosphere of the showroom building. Here are located the car displays, closing rooms, office and waiting rooms. In general, this is where the public will spend the greater percentage of its time. Here are located all personnel who have so-called 'white collar jobs'" (Cultum 1956: 13). And he goes on to say, "This business demands a special enclosure. It demands a building composite which will establish a congenial environment for selling automobiles and an efficient system for their maintenance" (6). It is important to note that the author recommends that the sales environment be "congenial," while the service side need only be "efficient." Fifty years later, attitudes about the physical design of dealerships remain much the same. While luxury is not a word that can be used to describe most automobile dealerships, the sales department usually makes an effort to provide a comfortable and pleasant place for its customers (and sales staff), while the service department has long had a reputation for customer (and staff) environments that are uncomfortable and unattractive. And in the areas designated as employee-only, the offices and workspaces tend to be bare bones, dreary, and colorless. Personal touches are rare.

Physically, the parts department is not an especially attractive place, and like other areas of the dealership that the customer does not see, dealers do not invest many resources in it. The counter area can sometimes appear messy and chaotic when the staff are in the middle of a number of tasks and assembling several orders, but the shelves are all neatly arranged and labeled, and everyone usually seems to know exactly where everything is. Many parts departments separate the technicians from the retail customers by having two counters. Technicians are the parts department's priority and are usually served first, so having a separate counter ensures that the retail customers are not aware of their slightly inferior status.

The shop is usually spacious with high ceilings and a variety of equipment scattered about the floor. The floor may be stained with oils or fuel. Computers and electronic diagnostic equipment, when not in use, are pushed against the wall. The atmosphere in the shop can be noisy, but it is fairly calm. Technicians usually work alone, focusing on the job at hand, although occasionally two technicians will work together when assisting each other with a difficult job or consulting about a problem.

The service advisors are usually standing at the front counter, facing the waiting room. They work very closely with other service advisors, who are all within a few feet of each other. Their work area is usually adjacent to the waiting room and is usually relatively pleasant and comfortable.

The sales area is clean, large, and spacious, with several highly polished vehicles placed around the room. Balloons, posters, and occasional plants add color to the space. A comfortable seating area with magazines and coffee is usually available to the customers. The salespeople's desks are located out on the floor, with the more private enclosed manager's offices off to the side.

In many GFC dealerships, the training environment is less than ideal and takes place in remote, small, unattractive rooms—not the kind of places in which one would look forward to spending time. This partially indicates the priority of training in dealerships, but it also reflects dealers' common attitude to the work environment and their employees—if customers do not see it, then it is not worth investing money in it. The training rooms can best be described as "out of sight, out of mind." The advantage of being far away from the sales or shop floor is that there are fewer distractions, but the disadvantage is that it is not easy to get to and it is easy to forget.

The Medium

INFORMATION TECHNOLOGY IN THE WORKPLACE

Though there has been a general expectation that information technology (IT) would revolutionize the workplace, there has been little agreement on the content of that revolution. As is often the case when projecting into the future, the technological future is seen in extremes. On one side, many have predicted a benign utopia in which technology liberates us from the drudgery of work, allows us greater control over our work environment, and decentralizes power. On the opposite, darker side, technology is seen as an alienating, dehumanizing, destructive, and sinister force used (intentionally or unintentionally) to oppress and control the workforce.

Early on in the era of mainframe computers, the assumption (and evidence) was that technology would centralize and reinforce the power of the already powerful, but as personal computers became common, that expectation was reversed. There is a long list of authors (such as Toffler 1980, Pool 1983; Barlow 1994; Negroponte 1995, Gates 1996; and Dertouzos 1997) who claim that information technology would decentralize power, enhance democracy, empower users, and generally improve the quality of our lives.

On the negative side, the subtitle of Harry Braverman's 1974 book *Labor and Monopoly Capital* says it all: *The Degradation of Work in the Twentieth Century*. He feared that because employers were only interested in the labor output of their workers, they would use technology to dehumanize the workplace and turn them into "electronic sweatshops." He was certainly not optimistic when he wrote, "The sad, horrible, heart-breaking way the vast majority of my fellow country men and women, as well as their counterparts in most of the rest of the world, are obliged to spend their working lives is seared into my consciousness in an excruciating and unforgettable way" (1974: xii). Though Braverman's view may seem a bit extreme, he certainly was not alone. Richard Edwards's *Contested Terrain: The Transformation of the Workplace in the Twentieth Century* (1979) also claimed that technology will never make the workplace democratic and will never be used to benefit workers or give them more control (viii). But even the most pessimistic authors take care to emphasize that it is not the technology itself that they object to, but rather the fact that technology is used to increase the employer's profit rather than for the betterment of the worker or society. For example, Paul Attewell in his essay "Big Brother and the Sweatshop" (1987) concludes that computer technology per se does not create sweatshop conditions. He argues that management has long had the surveillance tools to monitor who was a good or bad worker, but in spite of having the means, they have not turned clerical work into a sweatshop. They have not, not only because they do not wish to create that kind of work environment, but because the constraints that prevent them from doing so are numerous and complex.

Clearly, both the utopian and dystopian views are far too rigid to capture the subtle and multiple consequences of technological changes. In fact, as some authors point out (Barley 1988; Vallas 1990), both possibilities—good and evil—can coexist within the same firm or organization. And Barley also accurately notes that not only can new technology upset the work patterns and relationships among existing occupations and work groups, it can also spawn entirely new occupations.

Happily, in the past ten or fifteen years, the sweeping polarized views have moderated. Rather than trying to predict the future, researchers have turned to conducting empirical research on a wide range of topics, from the relationship between technology, skills, and jobs[4] to the effect of telecommunications on the city.[5] But the two topics that are of particular relevance to GFC's problem are IT adoption and using IT for communication.

ATTITUDES TOWARD IT ADOPTION

Much effort has also gone into investigating the adoption or diffusion of technology in firms and organizations. The tone of this literature varies in intensity, but in general, technology is assumed to be a positive force with the power to make even a lackluster firm more competitive and profitable. One gets the impression that other than in extreme situations, for example when surveillance is abusive, there are no good reasons to be unenthusiastic about a new technology. And because technology is seen as a sign of progress and modernity, those who resist are portrayed rather unsympathetically. Though most authors pay some lip service to the importance of "culture" and "organizational issues" that account for much of what happens in companies and organizations, there is always the lingering impression that the technology resisters are at fault. Companies who are able but do not quickly adopt new technologies are considered "laggards," and employees who resist are seen as backward, uncreative, and rigid—as we see in the Detroit office's view of GFC dealerships and their employees.

The most well-known group who rejected new technology was the early nineteenth-century Luddites, who rioted in the industrial regions of England and destroyed textile machines, to which they attributed high unemployment and low wages. *Neo-luddites* was a term coined in 1990 that referred to those who "resist the technology of the second Industrial Revolution [that is, computers] with the aim of protecting their lives which they see as on the verge of destruction" (Sale 1995: 237). Those who resisted the new digital technology were described by Ron Westrum in *Technologies and Society* (1991: 154) as fearful, insecure, or inflexible—not exactly the image to which most individuals or firms aspire.

Not all researchers make such harsh judgments however. For example, Orlikowski and Gash (1994), along with Guthrie and Dutton (1992) view technology not as an inexorable and ultimately irresistible external force, but as an artifact that is "situated" within a human and social environment, and where the artifact can only be understood by making sense of that environment and the artifact's place in it.[6] And technology being a social construct, different people react differently to it depending on their personal status, role, tenure, and individual characteristics (Orlikowski 1995).[7]

In terms of how organizations adopt or do not adopt new technology, Mohr (1982) states that there are two main approaches to the research on information-technology adoption in firms. The first tries to identify the environmental, organizational, and managerial characteristics that distinguish adopters from non-adopters and to predict the types of firms that will adopt technology.[8] The organizations that are early adopters of technology are considered to be risk-takers focused on gaining a competitive advantage, tolerant of ambiguity, persistent, team-oriented, flexible, open, collegial, capable of learning, sophisticated, and wealthy enough to have the surplus funds necessary to invest in a new technology. Moore and Benbasat (1991) added two important and relevant reasons why individuals or firms would or would not adopt a new technology: the degree to which the use of an innovation is perceived to enhance one's image or status in one's social system, and the degree to which use of the innovation is perceived as being voluntary. As we will see, both these reasons play an important part in the study of automobile dealerships.

The second approach to the research on IT adoption in organizations focuses on identifying the sequence of events that leads up to the decision to adopt a technology. But both approaches, whether focusing on characteristics or process, are unhelpful from a practical point of view because, as Langley and Truax (1994) and Fowler, García-Martín, Juristo, and Levine (1995) note, neither addresses how an organization can move from being a non-adopter to an adopter. New technology tends to be viewed as a simple matter of replacing or delivering new equipment or installing new software, when the real difficulties lie with the nontechnical issues—the human and organizational factors.

INFORMATION TECHNOLOGY SYSTEMS

Information technology (IT) is now an integral part of every dealership and its work practice, but its implementation has not been particularly smooth or happy. Each manufacturer has taken a slightly different path, but the experience of the GFC Motor Company illustrates how bumpy the road has been, and how early reasonable decisions can backfire, hindering the introduction and development of information and communication technologies in dealerships.

For GFC dealers in general, IT has been extremely expensive, and the systems have been difficult to use, with a rather confusing mix of equipment and software throughout the workplace. The inclination to use computers varies. "Some just aren't into it," one employee said. But others certainly are. One manager said, "Computer systems are like drugs to [some] dealers. It never ends; they can never get enough." The extent to which each individual dealership embraces information technology may vary, but most stores would typically have a variety of IT systems in place, especially in the service department.

GFC dealers' discontent with their computer systems began with imposed restrictions on what equipment they could buy and from whom they could buy it. Dealerships were permitted to buy equipment and software only from a few officially sanctioned companies, and because of these companies' monopoly, the prices they charged were high. Since the early 1990s, when the decision to limit dealers' choice in equipment procurement was made (a decision that actually made a great deal of sense at the time), the cost of hardware and software plummeted, and desktop computers became simpler and easier to use. Not surprisingly, dealers were resentful because they were prevented from taking advantage of these improvements and were obliged to buy what they considered to be antiquated, awkward, and expensive systems.[9]

In addition to the cost of the equipment, a medium- to large-sized GFC dealership would pay several thousand dollars per month to one of the companies for licensing, monthly fees, copy charges (for every page printed), hardware, software, and support. The general feeling was that everyone was making money off this arrangement, except for the dealers themselves.

The dealerships were unhappy with the cost of the hardware and software, but they were also not very pleased with some of the IT systems themselves. Staff complained that their computers could be difficult to use (at the time the systems tended to be DOS- or UNIX-based), slow, unreliable, limited, and inflexible (some applications would only allow one user at a time), while the manuals that came with the equipment were frequently unreadable. The consultants they had to hire for computer support were also expensive and often unhelpful. For example, one employee told the story of how he noticed that the dealership's monthly phone bills were enormous and realized that their computer system was calling long-distance instead of a local number to connect to their network. He called the company that installed the system and asked them to change it. They did, but the next month the phone bill was still very large. He then discovered that the consultant had come, but had only reprogrammed one machine with the correct telephone number, not the dozen located throughout the dealership. The technical consultant said that he had not corrected the others because no one had explicitly asked him to do so.

GFC dealerships have a confusing mix of computer equipment and applications, with the bulk of the technology located in the service department, especially the service bays and parts department.

The in-house system (purchased from one of the designated companies) is the workhorse of the dealership. It is text-based and not particularly user-friendly, but though the learning curve can be steep, employees certainly do learn to use it. It is used extensively by the service department to access customer information and the repair order database.[10]

There is a second online database that contains the latest in vehicle and service information for every vehicle manufactured and is used primarily by service advisors and technicians to diagnose problems. To use it, an employee has the computer dial Detroit and then types in the vehicle identification number[11] and a service code (a number representing the problem or symptom). The database then displays the latest updated information concerning that problem, including repair procedures.

Another technical information system used by the technicians offers publications, training courses on CD, and access to the online database in Detroit. A small shop might have one terminal placed in an easy-to-access location, but a large shop could have three or more. Most technicians like the system and use it frequently to get information about the vehicle they are repairing. The system contains service manuals, recall information, calibration information for reprogramming the diagnostic tools, and technical service bulletins. Technicians go to the machine, print out what they need, and then return to their workspaces. A related program, which is part of the online database system, was established to identify product problems early on. Its purpose is to encourage technicians to share with service engineers in Detroit what they have learned or identified as particular vehicle problems. The engineers can then begin to develop an appropriate repair procedure, which will be included in an updated version of the database. In spite of the system's good intentions, it is underused by technicians.

Technicians also have access to a diagnostic system that analyzes and interprets the diagnostic codes provided by the vehicle's sensors.[12] A technician inputs the vehicle's symptom and the diagnostic codes into the system and receives a problem diagnosis and suggested fix. Each system has more than a dozen standard test functions as well as a "customer flight recorder" and portable vehicle analyzer for diagnostic road testing. The one drawback to the system is that it is only available for late-model vehicles.

There is one final communication system that links the dealership with the manufacturer and is used primarily by the parts and sales departments. The parts department uses it to order parts every week, and salespeople use it to "build" a vehicle onscreen if they need to create a special order for a customer.

Because dealerships already had other information and communication systems in place at least since the late 1980s, they have been slower than most businesses to embrace the Internet. As of late 1999, some dealers had access to the Internet in some of their administrative offices, although it was rare to find Internet access in the service, parts, or sales departments. Since then, however, the situation has been changing very quickly.

There are other information and communication technologies used by any given dealership, including microfiche and CD-ROM in the parts department, but by far the technology of choice in all departments across all dealerships is the telephone. Almost every service advisor, parts employee, and salesperson spends much of their day on the telephone talking to customers and suppliers.

USE OF IT IN THE DEALERSHIP

In the parts department, telephones are the communication instrument of choice, but parts employees are also frequent computer users. A medium- to large-sized parts department typically would have several terminals for ordering parts. These terminals would link to the in-house system and access a database to check prices and availability of parts. A microfiche reader, which used to be standard equipment, is usually available as a backup in case the computers go down, or to access information about very old models. Two of the most frequently used resources are the CD with the diagrams of parts, and the parts locator. The diagrams, with their exploded illustrations of vehicle parts and assemblies, are invaluable for communicating with both technicians and customers to clarify which part or parts are needed, and to help identify the correct part number. The locator is used when the shop needs a part that is not in stock. The employee types the part number into the database, and the program lists the names and telephone numbers of the dealerships that have the part in stock, beginning with the dealerships that are geographically the closest. A quick telephone call verifies availability and facilitates payment and delivery.

The people in the sales department use much less information technology than their colleagues in the service department, but sales probably has felt and will continue to feel the greatest impact because of customers' increased use of computer technology and the Internet. Most sales departments use computers to some degree, but computers are slowly making an appearance on the salesperson's desk as well. In the past, the dearth of desktop computers was explained in terms of expense and lack of need. Inadequate training has also contributed to low confidence and has made many salespeople wary of the computer—they often claim that they are never sure what the machine is capable of doing. One person described the training provided by the computer firm that supplied the system as "hit and run."

Typically, the computers in the sales department will have access to the in-house system and perhaps Internet access, including e-mail. Salespeople use computers primarily for tracking customers, working out financial payments, arranging special orders, and retrieving product information. When customers come to the showroom, the salesperson is supposed to enter their names and addresses and the vehicles they are interested in into the in-house database. This serves several purposes. First, because most customers do not buy right away, the salesperson will need this information to contact them later in the week. It also protects the interests of the salesperson who first talked with the customer. Because most customers may visit the showroom several times before buying a car, it is very possible that the original salesperson will not be on duty when the customer decides to buy the vehicle. If the sale takes place within a week of a recorded phone call or within two weeks of a showroom visit, the original salesperson and the closing salesperson split the commission. In addition, it stops the customer who returns ready to buy from claiming a lower price if the original salesperson is off duty. The new salesperson simply calls up the information on the screen and verifies the original quote.

Managers also use the system to check that salespeople are doing the necessary follow-up with customers, and sales reps use it for working out lease and retail payments with their customers, looking up the trade-in value of a customer's car on the Kelly Blue Book Website, as well as "building" special order vehicles. If the manufacturer has a database of all the vehicles in stock in the area, salespeople can also use the system strategically. For example, if a customer from out of town comes in looking for a specific car in a particular color and the dealer has it in stock, the dealer can check the inventory of the local dealer in the customer's hometown (knowing that the customer will go there if he or she has not already). If the other dealer does not have the car, the first dealer knows he or she can push the price slightly higher.

And of course the dealerships that have contracts with some of the online vehicle purchasing companies, such as Autobytel, would likely have a dedicated computer for that purpose. Autobytel dealers pay Autobytel for exclusive rights over a certain geographic area. If the customer goes to the Autobytel site and states an interest in a certain type of vehicle, Autobytel e-mails the dealer with the customer's contact information. The salesperson will e-mail the customer back with a quote (usually 1 percent over invoice) and urge the customer to come in for a test drive. Though the markup is low on these vehicles, salespeople hope to compensate by receiving bonuses for sales volume. In 1999 online sales were still in their early stages, with an Autobytel dealer receiving 50–60 requests per month, which might lead to 6–8 purchases—but the scene is rapidly changing. As of January 2000, Autobytel began selling cars over the Internet, bypassing the dealer completely (Meredith 2000).

The rapid growth of use of the Internet in everyday life has had a great effect on the work inside the dealership. In addition to creating a more knowledgeable customer, it has increased competition. Not only must dealers continue to compete with their local competitors, they have to also outbid the new online dealerships. Salespeople are becoming nervous about this trend, and they are particularly worried about the possibility of the manufacturers bypassing them and selling directly to the consumer online.

DISTANCE EDUCATION SYSTEM

Facing increasing competition, a greater emphasis on customer satisfaction, and greater technical sophistication of vehicles, GFC saw increased dealership staff training as key to maintaining its competitive advantage. In the past, dealership employees were trained at regional training centers—a rather expensive and time-consuming undertaking. The problem was that a third of the dealerships were more than a hundred miles from the nearest training center, and they could not increase training without requiring their employees to spend significant amounts of time away from the workplace. They needed to find a system that could provide more training to employees, yet at the same time reduce the amount of time employees spent away from the workplace. Their solution was to broadcast daily live training from Detroit to every GFC dealership via satellite through the Distance Education System (DES).[13] DES was not intended to replace hands-on skills however; training still takes place in dozens of training centers located throughout North America. Currently, approximately 25 percent of all courses are classroom-facilitated, and about 75 percent are delivered via DES, CD-ROM, or self-study.

Growing quickly since it first began in the mid-1990s, the DES broadcasts over sixty hours of live training programs each day from Detroit studios, on seven channels, to U.S. and Canadian dealerships. Topics range from "Improving Parts Operations" to "Technical Training for Non-Technical Personnel" to "Selling to Women." For example, in one month alone, DES offered twenty-three different technical classes and another twenty-two classes on parts and service operations. There were additional orientation classes to teach users about the functionality of DES (including distance learning, e-mail, and personal computing), thirteen classes for parts managers, thirty-five classes in sales, and another twelve on general topics.

A typical DES system broadcasts a signal from a studio in Detroit to a satellite that bounces it back to its target destination on earth within a half-second. Each dealership is equipped with a dish antenna to receive the signal, an earth station, a monitor to display the broadcast, and several keypads for the students to use to interact with the instructor.

The system is two-way data, one-way video, and one-way voice. Interactivity is limited. Participants at a dealership receiving the broadcast can see and hear the live broadcast on the monitor, but they have only limited voice and data links back to Detroit. The instructor cannot see the students, and the calls from the participants in the dealerships to Detroit are sent over standard telephone lines. Most of the interactivity occurs through the keypad—instructors pose multiple-choice questions to the group, and the students respond by pressing the appropriate key on the keyboard. The responses are tabulated instantly for the instructor, who can then display the results on the screen for the participants. To speak to the instructor, a student presses the call button on the keypad, and if the person is chosen to speak, his or her voice is patched through via telephone lines and broadcast to all participants.

Instructor's studio desks are located in Michigan, Canada, Australia, and Mexico, with the majority in Detroit. Each studio desk consists of an overhead projector, cameras, tape machines, a writing tablet, monitors, computers, and controllers, and requires only one instructor and a technical assistant per program. In front of the instructor are three monitors: one for the Web, another for multiple-choice questions, and a third with a touch screen for controlling the nine possible camera shots. The instructor touches on the view or camera shot he or she prefers, and it is instantly shown on the monitor.

Content: Learning and Communication

LEARNING IN THE WORKPLACE

As human beings, we all learn, whether informally or formally, and learning is a concept with which we are very familiar. However, as a society we tend to define learning and education rather narrowly. As schoolchildren we learned that learning is synonymous with taking in information and being able to produce the right answer. Traditionally, we see education as the one-way delivery of information and subsequent absorption by the learner. But the ability to parrot back the right answer to a teacher is not what is required in the workplace. Instead, workers are being asked to learn in order to do their jobs better, to think, and to respond creatively to new challenges. As Peter Senge has stated (1996), transforming old habits and learning how to learn in the workplace is not an easy process, and we should not be surprised when employees show little intrinsic motivation to learn—that is, to experiment and discover new insights from mistakes and outcomes that do not turn out according to plan.

American firms spend billions each year—$50 billion in 1998 according to the U.S. Department of Labor—on formal training in the workplace. GFC, like the other automobile companies, has invested millions of dollars in training for dealership employees. Though training has always been important, it became an even higher priority in the 1990s because of changes in the industry, which included a greater emphasis on customer satisfaction, increased competition, and greater technical sophistication of vehicles. GFC saw highly trained dealership staff as key to maintaining its competitive advantage and future success.

Though American firms spend billions each year on formal training in the workplace, between 62 percent and 83 percent of actual employee learning takes place informally (Marsick and Watkins 1990; Verespej 1998; EDC 1998). Despite its prevalence, informal learning often receives less attention because it is thought of as an intangible form of learning, difficult to define and quantify (Garrick 1998). Informal learning is usually described by what it is not, and is simply defined as the opposite of formal learning (Figure 4.2). Typically it is not institutionally sponsored, classroom-based, or highly structured. It is also characterized by greater control by the learner over the content and context (Marsick and Watkins 1990). There is also some disagreement about whether or not it is a deliberate act by the employee. Some define informal learning as nonintentional, but it can also be planned, for example, in the case of self-directed learning or when help is consciously and

Formal Learning	Informal Learning	
	Intentional Learning	**Incidental Learning**
• Institutionally-sponsored	• Noninstitutional	• Nonintentional
• Classroom-based	• Non-classroom	• Often a by-product of some other activity
• Highly structured	• Learner controlled	• Examples:
	• Examples:	Mistakes
	Self-directed learning	Interpersonal interactions
	Networking	Workplace culture
	Coaching	Experimentation
	Mentoring	Hidden curriculum of
	Trial-and-error	formal learning

Figure 4.2. Definitions of formal and informal learning

directly sought from fellow employees, advisors, coaches, or mentors. To make the distinction, nonintentional learning is often called "incidental learning" and is considered a subcategory of informal learning. Incidental learning is defined as a by-product of task accomplishment, interpersonal interaction, organizational culture, or trial-and-error experimentation. It is never intentional, seldom explicit, and almost always serendipitous, and is buried in the context of other tasks (Marsick and Watkins 1990: 6–8).

Informal learning can take place almost anywhere—in organizations that deliberately encourage it and all along the spectrum to an environment that is not highly conducive to learning. And though informal learning is thought to take place between employees, Marsick and Watkins quite rightly point out that learning can also occur between customers and employees.

A good example of informal learning and how effective it can be is described in Julian Orr's *Talking About Machines* (1996). Xerox technicians recount "war stories" as the principle means of staying informed of what is going on in their field, the subtleties of machine behavior, and problematic situations. These narratives serve to demonstrate the technician's mastery of dealing with machines and of the only somewhat less difficult art of dealing with customers. Told informally over lunch or coffee get-togethers, "war stories" allow other technicians to learn from the experiences of their colleagues.

Though informal learning may be prevalent and important, what exactly are employees learning? According to the EDC report (1998) there are four types of work skills that employees learn informally, and all four can be found in GFC dealerships:

- Practical skills (such as job-specific knowledge, safety issues)

- Intrapersonal skills (such as problem solving, critical thinking, stress management, prioritizing)

- Interpersonal skills (such as communication skills, presentation skills, teamwork, conflict resolution)

- Cultural awareness (such as teamwork dynamics, professional advancement, social norms, and priorities)

Informal learning may be more common than formal, and it may deserve more attention than it traditionally receives, but it certainly should not be seen as a substitute for formal learning. In fact, the two are strongly interconnected. One study estimated that every hour of formal training yields a four-hour spillover of informal learning (Stamps 1998). For an example of how this formal-informal relationship plays out in the workplace, consider the hypothetical scenario in which GFC engineers have figured out how to retrofit a new type of air bag in an older model of vehicle. They would create a formal DES training program in conjunction with the training department, and an individual technician would then take the class and learn how this somewhat tricky installation is done. In the course of the next year, if the technician who works in the adjacent service bay is trying to install new air bags, the technician who participated in the DES program could take a few moments to walk over to demonstrate to his colleague how the job is done. In this way, the second technician would informally learn how to correctly install the air bags. But what if they discover that this particular model is slightly unusual and the solution learned from the DES program does not strictly apply? Together they could find a solution to the problem and install the air bags properly and efficiently. If the system is working well, the individual technicians who learned how to solve the problem of installing air bags in that model of car would contact GFC engineers in Detroit to inform them of their solution, which would then be fed into the organizational memory and incorporated into the "Helpline" database as well as into future formal DES programming and technical training.

ORGANIZATIONAL LEARNING AND LEARNING ORGANIZATIONS

As stated earlier, the GFC Motor Company wanted to increase organizational learning within the firm and believed that this could be done by broadcasting training programs, distributing information, and encouraging two-way communication between Detroit and the dealerships. The desire to dramatically increase learning and communication within the firm is not particularly unique. Authors have been writing about organizational learning for over thirty years (Sligo 1996: 508), but the real momentum began in the late 1980s. By the mid-1990s the perceived need for organizational learning within firms was well-accepted, as evidenced by Peter Senge's 1990 book *The Fifth Discipline: The Art and Practice of the Learning Organization*, followed up by *The Fifth Discipline Fieldbook* in 1994.

A sizable literature on organizational learning has accumulated and, as Argyris and Schön (1978, 1996) note, it can generally be divided into two separate branches. One is normative, practice-oriented, enthusiastic, and largely uncritical. The second branch tends to be more distant from practice, as well as skeptical, neutral, and nonprescriptive.[14] In their own work, however, Argyris and Schön tried to take the middle ground by focusing on individual practitioners whom they saw as centrally important, because they believed that it was an individual's thinking and actions that influenced learning at the organizational level.

A term closely related to *organizational learning* is *learning organization*, and the words are sometimes used interchangeably.[15] Both terms are somewhat ambiguous, and the relationship between them is not very clear. Tsang (1997: 75) tries to clarify the difference by saying that *organizational learning* is a concept used to describe certain types of activity that take place in an organization while *learning organization* refers to a particular type of organization. And, he says, there is a simple relationship between the two—a learning organization is simply one that is good at organizational learning. However, a clear definition and consensus on the concept of a learning organization have proved to be elusive over the years (Garvin 1993; Tsang 1997).[16] For example, Gephart, Marsick, Van Buren, and Spiro (1996: 36) define a learning organization as an organization that has an enhanced capacity to learn, adapt, and change. It is an organization in which learning processes are analyzed, monitored, developed, managed, and aligned with improvement and innovation goals. Huber (1996: 822) states that an organization learns when, through its processing of information, it increases the probability that its future actions will lead to improved performance. Lipshitz, Popper, and Oz (1996: 293–294) define organizational learning as a cultural rather than a cognitive phenomenon, and a process through which organization members develop shared values and knowledge based on past experience of themselves and others. In short, the concept of learning organizations is based on a commitment to collective learning and development (Snell 2001).

Although much of the rhetoric exhorts companies to become learning organizations, it is relatively uninformative on how to develop this capacity. Many authors seem certain that they know one when they see one, and offer a laundry list of essential features.[17] Robin Snell (2001) offers a more concise list of characteristics: free exchange in, across, and between communities of practice; networked knowledge and experience; continual improvement; learning leadership; open dialogue; continual transformation; and "protean" psychological contracts (meaning that members' growth and competence are enhanced by exposing them to challenges, support, and the fostering of developmental relationships).[18]

Another description by Lipshitz et al. (1996: 295) states that a learning organization is characterized by its culture. It will show appreciation for and willingness to invest resources in learning activities (continuous learning); show appreciation for and willingness to incur losses to obtain valid information; be willing to expose one's operations to inspection (transparency); judge the actions and opinions of organizational members on their merit and not according to the members' rank, prestige, or any other personal attribute (egalitarianism); and take personal responsibility for implementing lessons learned (accountability).

Although the terms may seem ambiguous, the important point is that rigid hierarchy and following orders are no longer considered to be admirable or effective ways of running an organization. In a twenty-first century, dynamic environment, in order to be successful both individuals and organizations must be flexible, open to change, and able to learn and adapt.[19] How they get there, what they look like, the work they do, and the environment that they operate in will vary with the organization. Though the promotion of learning organizations is often targeted at businesses, advocates believe that all organizations, including nonprofits, schools, and even governments, could and should actively learn from their mistakes and successes, and continually innovate if they are to remain competitive.

BARRIERS TO CREATING A LEARNING ORGANIZATION

In spite of the logic and enthusiasm for learning organizations, creating one is not a simple task—structural, procedural, and cultural barriers can easily thwart efforts, as GFC clearly illustrates.

The culture of an organization poses one of the largest barriers and can include a narrow definition of learning and education, a lack of incentives and motivation, fear and negative attitudes, and false expectations. Dilworth (1996) argues that there are five principal cultural barriers to creating learning organizations: (1) treatment of learning as an individual phenomenon rather than as something that can involve a group of people; (2) fixation on formal training, with little attention given to informal workplace learning; (3) treating business and learning processes as entirely discrete worlds; (4) non-listening work environments—non-listening effectively blocks communication and the kinds of idea interchange necessary to promote organizational learning; and (5) autocratic leadership styles, which can lead to an atmosphere of distrust, fear, blocked communications, fragmentation of work effort, and stultification of organizational learning.

ENCOURAGING LEARNING IN THE WORKPLACE

In spite of a generally accepted assumption that learning, especially informal learning, is valuable in an organization, pinpointing the exact conditions needed to encourage it is more of a challenge. David Stamps (1998) uses the term *learning ecologies*, while Nardi and O'Day (1999) use *information ecologies* to describe the mix of interdependent elements and cultural factors that cause informal learning to happen, or not happen. Using the term *ecology* is useful because not only does it convey the complexity involved, it reminds us that it is something that cannot be totally managed or controlled.

As with the literature on learning organizations, authors are often able to describe the characteristics of a firm that encourages informal learning. For example, a "good" organization that is learning-friendly usually has a culture of openness and trust, and recognizes the efforts of employees, which in turn motivates them to learn. On the other hand, a "bad" firm is characterized by unilateral control, secrecy, and win-lose thinking. Unfortunately there are few suggestions on how to become a "good" firm, or how, for example, to shift from a culture of secrecy to one of openness.

There is a tight link between individual and organizational learning, because organizations can only learn if individual employees learn. The organization may have created the conditions to encourage learning, but the individual employee must also be ready and able to learn. Those who take advantage of learning informally from interactions with others are seen positively. Marsick and Watkins (1990) describe these individuals as proactive, with the ability to reflect critically and creatively.

Despite all the reservations about the usefulness of the concept and the severe challenges organizations face in becoming learning organizations, most authors would agree that learning usually, though not always, increases an organization's and individual's capacities to perform better. An organization that is quick to correct its errors and react to environmental changes should, on average, outperform one that seldom learns from past mistakes. And this is what GFC aspired to.

SITUATED LEARNING AND COMMUNITIES OF PRACTICE

Two more relevant concepts that are important to briefly review are "situated learning" and "communities of practice." In the late 1980s, Lucy Suchman introduced the idea of situated practice in *Plans and Situated Actions* (1987), and four years later Jean Lave and Etienne Wenger developed the concept of situated learning (1991). Both are based on the idea that learning and practice are quintessentially social in nature. The situated learning approach differs quite radically from the traditional view of learning, which is normally considered a one-way, and usually solitary, absorption process. In contrast, situated learning redirects the focus from the individual to the world around the learner and the relationship of the learner to that world. From the perspective of situated learning, a worker does not just absorb new information while he or she learns, but in fact becomes a different person through the social processes involved.[20]

An example of situated learning is the process by which a new employee begins on the periphery of the workgroup but gradually joins in as he or she learns and gains skills and experience.[21] An apprentice, or the new service advisor, is a good example of someone who engages in this process. Beginning work on the outside edge of the group is advantageous because there is less intensity, less risk, more assistance, and less production pressure. Eventually the new employee becomes a full participant, engaging with the technologies of everyday practice as well as participating in the social relations, activities, and production processes of the group, and gradually becomes a full member of the workgroup (Lave and Wenger 1991; Wenger 1998: 100).

Thinking about learning in the workplace as a social process is extremely helpful because it makes the connection between individual and organizational learning. Instead of looking at the individual *or* the organization, it melds the two and places the individual within the social and cultural world of an organization's workplace.

Communities of practice is a term that puts learning organizations into more of a sociocultural context. It was first coined by Jean Lave and Etienne Wenger and defined as "a set of relations among persons, activity, and world, over time, and in relation with other tangential and overlapping communities of practice" (1991: 98). The concept of community of practice is largely "an intuitive notion" (42), but the core meaning encompasses the concept that *work and learning are social activities and work is framed by the culture in which the employees are situated.* The term is used broadly to refer to groups collaboratively working together and actively learning from each other. A community of practice is not a synonym for a group, a team, or a network, however. It is neither a social category nor a geographical location. As Wenger (1998) states, calling every imaginable social configuration a community of practice would render the concept meaningless, as would encumbering it with too restrictive a definition. To him, communities of practice possess sustained mutual relationships; a rapid flow of information and propagation of innovation; an absence of introductory preambles; specific tools, representations, and other artifacts; local lore and certain styles recognized as displaying membership; and a shared discourse reflecting a certain perspective on the world. In short, communities of practice typically possess three primary characteristics. They have a stock of common shared knowledge, they develop shared values and attitudes, and they possess a sense of collective or group identity (Hislop 2003: 166).

We all belong to communities of practice, and they are an integral part of our daily lives, but they are so informal and so pervasive that they rarely come into explicit focus. Communities of practice are also the building blocks of learning organizations. And Wenger also reminds us that communities of practice are not automatically positive. They can also be the source of problems, such as exclusion and narrowness, as much as a key to solutions.

In the 2002 book, *Cultivating Communities of Practice*, Wenger, McDermott, and Snyder seem to broaden the definition somewhat by describing a community of practice as a set of people who "share a concern, a set of problems, or a passion about a topic, who deepen their knowledge and expertise in this area by interacting on an ongoing basis" (4). The authors also suggest ways that communities of practice can be cultivated: "Organizations can do a lot to create an environment in which they can prosper: valuing the learning they do, making time and other resources available for their work, encouraging participation, and removing barriers. Creating such a context also entails integrating communities in the organization—giving them a voice in decisions and legitimacy in influencing operating units, and developing internal processes for managing the value they create" (13).

FORMAL AND INFORMAL LEARNING IN THE DEALERSHIP

As discussed in the DES section of this chapter, there is an impressive assortment of training programs offered each week in any given GFC dealership. Though over sixty hours and a wide range of programs are broadcast daily, only one program can be viewed at a time, so a certain amount of planning is required, usually by an employee in the dealership who is designated as the DES coordinator. Classes range from the technical ("Power Sliding Doors," "Brake and Noise Vibration") to management ("Resolving Customer Concerns," "Leadership for Managers") to financing ("Leasing," "Credit") to sales ("Greeting the Customer," "Win-Win Negotiating").

Recently a policy was introduced requiring all employees to be certified, which means they must attend certain classes and pass a test each year, in order to keep their jobs.[22] The number of classes employees have to take each year is not onerous—often only one or two—but employees are encouraged to take more than the minimum number of classes, either on their own time or with the permission of their supervisor.

To participate, an employee registers with the Detroit office for a specific class, and the workbooks arrive some weeks later. At the appropriate time, the employee goes to the room where the equipment is located, turns on the equipment, sets it to the appropriate channel, and types in his or her ID number. A database keeps track of the training each person has received.

A typical broadcast lasts two hours. The first fifteen to twenty minutes are usually spent on administrative matters (for example, how to use the equipment, which version of the workbook should be used, and phone numbers to call for help). The instructor, who is referred to as the "host," is usually a person with many years of experience who has held the same position as the participants (technicians teach technicians, salespeople teach salespeople,

and so on). The host then administers a short survey (the number of participants can range from a dozen to several hundred) in order to find out what
jobs the students hold and how long they have been in the automotive industry. Participants respond by pressing the appropriate keys on their keypads. The answers are tabulated and displayed on the screen for everyone to
see. The class then begins. The host covers the material, often requesting
that the audience call in and talk about their own experiences, and occasionally stops to give a multiple-choice quiz. There is usually a ten-minute break
at the halfway point. The class then continues after the break, often repeating some of the material presented in the first half.

The broadcasts are usually quite professional in scope and presentation.
The producers and hosts are knowledgeable about the material, and they put
a great deal of effort into creating their sessions.[23] The pop-quizzes and surveys work well too, with feedback tabulated almost instantaneously. The interaction part of the program, however, leaves much to be desired. Two-way
conversation is technically awkward, and the comments from the participants tend to be banal. To communicate with the host (and fellow students),
a participant pushes a call button on the keypads, which calls up Detroit over
the telephone lines. When the host wishes to speak to the caller, the call is
patched into the broadcast for others to hear. In theory, this could be an excellent way for dealership employees to contribute and share their experience with others—and sometimes it is. Too often though, calls do not go
through, or the calls that do connect are from people who have pushed their
call buttons only to say once they are on air, "I was just seeing if this thing
worked." Instead of being exciting and informative, the interaction is more
often disruptive and boring.

The sessions are broadcast during the workday, beginning at 8:00 A.M.
and continuing until 8:00 P.M. This scheduling obviously makes sense because most dealerships operate during these hours, but they are also the
hours when the employees are the busiest. It is technically possible to tape
the broadcasts to watch at a later time, but from the head office's perspective
the person would not have taken the course because he or she did not log on
or take the test at the end of the class, and therefore the program could not
count toward certification.

Though the DES training system has not been warmly embraced, it has
been accepted, albeit somewhat unenthusiastically. One person called it "an

evil necessity." In hindsight, many employees look back at the training in regional centers with fondness because they enjoyed the change in routine,
and many claim that they learned more with the face-to-face interaction of
the classes. Of course they will also admit that their complaints about training are not new or unique to DES—they used to also gripe about being sent
off to classes at the training centers.

There are four main complaints that GFC dealership employees have
about the DES training system. First, they are so busy and their days are so
hectic that it is hard to find the time for classes. For example, the employees
in the parts department say that the programs are not very convenient for
them because their busiest time is from 10:00 A.M. to 3:00 P.M., which is the
same time that the majority of the parts-oriented programs are scheduled.
Shorter classes held at the end of the day would be a welcome improvement
for them. Related to this is the problem of scheduling—managers have to
plan weeks in advance when their staff will take the classes, but they never
know if that day will be particularly quiet or chaotic. As a consequence,
many end up postponing their training until the end of the year.[24] The current system simply does not allow managers to be spontaneous and take advantage of the training when they have an unexpected lull in their workday.

Dealership managers have questioned whether DES training should be
available at home with more emphasis on self-study, but reactions have been
mixed: some employees liked the idea that the classwork could be done away
from the dealership while others were adamant that any training should take
place at work and not at home. After all, they argue, the staff already work
very long hours, and when they do get home, it should be a break from
work, not an extension of it. One employee explained that though he thought
the option of self-study was good, it was impractical in his own case because
after nine hours of work not only was he exhausted, but he also had to take
care of family and household responsibilities.

The second problem is matching the classes to the skills and experience
of the employees. Only the courses for technicians are rated according to
degree of difficulty. For the rest of the employees, introductory classes bore
the more experienced person, and yet a more advanced class would probably
overwhelm a new employee with little dealership experience. A related problem is matching the course to the learning styles of the participants: some individuals are much more comfortable learning by hearing new material,

some rely more heavily on visuals, and others learn best by actually doing or practicing the skill rather than reading or hearing about it.

Another complaint has to do with the pay structure within the dealerships. Not all dealerships pay their employees for the hours spent in training. Many dealers do pay their employees an hourly rate for training, but those employees who are paid partially or completely by commission (service advisors, parts counter employees, and salespeople), as well as the technicians who are paid a flat rate, obviously will make less money during training than they can on the sales or shop floor. In a culture that rewards its employees almost exclusively through their paycheck, this is quite a disincentive.

And finally, GFC dealership employees complain about the logistics, management, and organization of the classes, particularly the call-in segment. Almost everyone who takes the classes says that they like the idea of hearing from others doing the same job in other dealerships, but they dislike and resent the high number of callers who waste everyone's time by either calling in to check their equipment or having nothing interesting to say.

Training for dealership employees is not limited to the DES broadcasts. In the training room there is usually a desktop PC with a CD-ROM used by technicians to take courses as part of their certification, courses that are often used in preparation for off-site training. The sales department relies mostly on DES training for upgrading skills, but the manufacturer still organizes half-day motivational events and new-product seminars off-site.

Of all the employees, service advisors are the most active recipients of on-the-job training and informal learning. Unlike the service technicians, experienced service advisors are routinely asked to teach a new employee.[25] The standard training procedure is to have new service advisors sit with the other advisors and slowly absorb what they need to know over a period of several weeks. As they become familiar with the system, they will start with simple tasks and build up to more complex ones. (New trainees say learning the computer and the codes are the most challenging.) After about four or five weeks, the new service advisor should be able to perform most tasks independently, but it is an ongoing process, with advisors continually learning from their colleagues, and refining and updating their knowledge. New advisors will obviously ask more questions and need more assistance than their experienced colleagues.[26]

In dealerships where the service advisors are within earshot of the service manager, even more teaching and learning goes on. It is very common for a manager to informally monitor the advisors' conversations and to call out a quick answer or suggestion when necessary. Or, if the situation calls for a more lengthy explanation, the manager will call the employee into the office to talk.

The technicians in the shop use the most extensive array of computers and information technology in the dealership, and apparently they have adapted to it relatively easily. As one service manager noted, "Lots of cars are fixed now without picking up a wrench." In the service bay area, technicians have access to a number of services, including the in-house database, diagnostic equipment, electronic documentation, and online databases. How often technicians use these tools depends on the type of work they are doing, as well as on the individual—some may use it on a daily basis, others only once a month. In addition, the opportunities for ongoing formal training through the Distance Education System and other training programs are extensive, and the technicians, along with the parts employees, appear to be quite agreeable to training in general. Their greater enthusiasm stems from the clear and direct benefits that they receive from the training. For them it is a simple formula: the more they know about new vehicles and vehicle repair, the more they can earn.

Informal learning and on-the-job training for technicians are extremely important and are by far the most prevalent. When problems are not easily diagnosed or repaired, the technician will sometimes have to ask for help. First, he will check the repair manuals, technical bulletins, and databases. If that is unsuccessful, he may ask for help informally. Even though the service bays are noisy and technicians usually work far enough apart to make conversation difficult, they still are able to exchange information and learn from each other. In addition, though not encouraged by management, if technicians have a problem or are puzzled about something, instead of ordering their parts via computer, they will walk over to the parts counter and order them in person. While they wait for their order to be filled, they have a few minutes to casually ask about the problem they are having. Co-workers who may have had a similar experience will offer tips and suggestions, or sometimes simply sympathy for the frustration of a troublesome job.

Sometimes the training is informal, but intentional. Senior technicians can be assigned to work with inexperienced ones, though this is not always a satisfactory arrangement because young technicians can sometimes interpret the help and training as criticism, and the more experienced technicians sometimes resent having to spend time away from their own work. Encouraging individual and peer-to-peer learning can be a fairly subtle process. In one shop, the dispatcher knowingly assigns less-experienced technicians to work on jobs that are a little too difficult for them. He first lets them try by themselves for a while, but then he will ask an expert technician to help. When the work is completed (by the learner), the expert technician double-checks to make sure that the work was done correctly. The dispatcher then splits the billable time for the job between the learner and the expert technician so that the expert is paid for the time spent teaching.

And if the problem still cannot be diagnosed or solved in-house, they will then contact the manufacturer. The technical support engineers based in Detroit typically specialize in a particular concern or type of vehicle, are highly skilled in diagnostics, and usually have a bachelor's degree in automotive technology as well as extensive practical experience. Finally, if they are unable to resolve the problem, the case is forwarded to the regional office, and an engineer is sent to the dealership to work side-by-side with the technician.

Though the reaction to formal training varies with the individual, the average dealership employee could be described as fairly resigned and accepting. But that average would also hide the quite significant differences in attitude between the service and sales department to learning and training. The service department employees appear to be much more open to training in general, and DES in particular. One service manager said that as far as he was concerned, "The more training, the better." Technicians and parts employees, for example, seemed to have the least objection to the training, perhaps because theirs is more straightforward and focuses on the nuts and bolts (literally and figuratively) of doing their jobs. They are quite aware that knowing more about the vehicles will help them work faster and ultimately earn more.

This is in stark contrast to the attitude in the sales department, where employees are reluctant participants in training programs and are particularly unenthused about the DES broadcasts. It was a salesman, for example, who stomped up the stairs to the training room bellowing in a loud and angry voice for the benefit of all to hear, "I'd like to get a hold of a rocket and blow up the satellite so that I wouldn't have to do this [expletive] anymore." Other salespeople are somewhat less dramatic, but still refer to their required training as "doing time." This very negative reaction is puzzling given that the training and testing requirements for salespeople are some of the least demanding. Often they only have to complete one training program per year, and the annual certification is not particularly challenging, entailing a series of four open-book tests; as one manager explained, "If you can read, you can pass them."

What then could explain the strong reaction to training requirements that are neither demanding nor onerous? There are a number of possibilities worth considering.

First, the formal classes constantly emphasize the need to change the salespeople's views and attitudes toward customers. They are forever being told that they must be more polite, accommodating, and straightforward with the customer. It must be particularly irritating for the older salespeople who may have been doing this job (successfully) for years because the trainers' exhortations imply that the salespeople have been "wrong" all this time. Of all the employees, the salespeople are the ones whose jobs are based on their relationship with the customer, and any potential change or upset to this delicate balance could threaten them, their view of themselves, and their livelihood.[27]

Salespeople also resent the classes because it takes them off the sales floor. Other dealership employees may suffer financially somewhat during training sessions—service advisors and technicians would receive their standard hourly pay, but miss out on any commission—but salespeople potentially have a much higher financial penalty because every hour spent in a class is an hour not selling vehicles. And if they are not selling vehicles, they are not earning an income. Of course, this is a *potential* penalty only, because an average salesperson would only sell a vehicle every two or three days, not every hour. But more to the point, many salespeople will say that they spend the two-hour classes worrying that they are missing the thing they really love— making a terrific sale out on the showroom floor.

Sales staff are "people" people. They thrive on face-to-face contact with others, so sitting in a room by themselves watching a television monitor is one of their least preferred environments. They do not mind attending off-site training courses quite as much (even though it also means not being able to sell cars) because such training offers face-to-face experience and is usually their only chance of meeting other sales reps in the region. As one salesperson commented, he enjoyed the off-site training sessions because he was always able to pick up a tip or two from listening to others.

Finally, and possibly most important, formal training is not embraced because of the salespeople's fundamental belief that sales cannot be taught, that the ability to sell is both mysterious and innate. People either have "the right stuff" or they don't. The belief in some individuals' natural ability to sell does not contradict the sales managers' efforts to train their sales staff in proper techniques. The right technique will enable an average person to be fairly successful in selling cars, but having that mysterious quality makes a truly great salesperson. Salespeople maintain that no class or training session can teach you how to acquire that mysterious quality.

And, as always, there are exceptions. Most dealerships have at least one salesperson (who is considered an aberration by his or her colleagues) who thoroughly enjoys the training programs and will go out of his or her way to take more than the required courses.

In the past, dealerships commonly took a rather Darwinian approach to training new hires. They would hire ten new sales reps when only one was needed, and these new employees would be "thrown to the wolves" or "thrown to the lions." If they survived by outselling the others, they could keep their jobs. The others were fired. Salespeople who have been through this process say with some pride that they were trained in "the school of hard knocks." Obviously those who did not thrive as a result of this teaching technique are long gone from the dealership.

Today though, most dealerships no longer employ such cutthroat techniques, and they tend to make more of an effort to hire a suitable person and then provide some kind of basic but fairly informal training, usually put together by the sales manager and sometimes an outside consultant. The training period may last four to ten days, but five is the norm, after which the new employees are expected to be on the floor selling full time. During this introductory period they are introduced to the basics of selling (some roleplaying and learning what to say at each step of the process) and are taught how to fill out forms. They must familiarize themselves with the vehicles through printed material, self-study materials, videotapes, and test drives. In addition they learn dealership-specific information such as using the computer system and the route they should follow when taking customers for a test drive. When asked about their training program, one sales manager said he "shows them the location of the keys [to the vehicles on the lot], the lunchroom, and the men's room." Though said in jest, there is a certain amount of truth to it.

Again, this lack of interest in training, whether it be formal or informal, largely stems from the salespeople's belief that sales cannot be taught. As one person said, "You can teach cars, but not sales." Though there are tips and techniques that can be learned, the essential act of selling a car—that raw human-to-human communication—is not something that can be taught.

Unlike the employees in the service and parts departments, experienced sales reps are not expected or encouraged to teach new employees. Pairing a new salesperson with an experienced salesperson is rarely done. Supposedly this would make customers feel uncomfortable, but that it makes the salespeople uncomfortable is probably closer to the truth. Because sales reps are in active competition with each other, the chances of a senior salesperson sharing knowledge, experience, and successful sales techniques with a beginner is unlikely. They do, however, often allow new employees to sit in during delivery of the car—the time when the salesperson reviews maintenance schedules, driving tips, and warranty conditions with the new customer. Apparently, once the customer has bought the vehicle, bringing in a second salesperson is less alarming. And of course, the sales commission has already been safely made.

Though the introductory training for new sales employees may be limited, daily on-the-job training does take place. The floor sales manager's desk is often a central point in the showroom where all salespeople must go to have their offers approved, and where they gather to chat if business is slow. From this position, the sales manager can act as a coach, supervisor, mediator, and teacher, constantly increasing the sales staff's knowledge of the car business, selling techniques, product information, and customer relations. Though this process is informal and rarely recognized or acknowledged as training, salespeople probably learn more about the business and the process of selling vehicles from their sales managers than from any other source.

Individuals also learn through trial-and-error, experimenting with different sales approaches and techniques to discover what works and what does not work for them. In addition, successful sales reps say that if a person is a good listener, he or she can learn a lot from customers, who are often very knowledgeable about a particular type of vehicle.

Though peer-to-peer informal learning is often not expected or actively encouraged in a dealership, it certainly does take place, and it is not always positive. Some service managers complain about lazy employees with bad attitudes who "contaminate" the other employees by teaching them their own bad habits. Another example was given by a sales rep who observed that new and inexperienced salesmen often arrived at the dealership with a fairly positive, or at least neutral, attitude toward women. Unfortunately though, within a few months of being steeped in the showroom culture and learning from "the old guys," they too gradually became condescending, disrespectful, and rude toward their female customers and fellow employees.

COMMUNICATION AND IT

Communication is at the core of learning, whether it is individual, organizational, or social. And technology, whether it is the telephone, telegraph, radio, television, or Internet, has long been used to assist and extend communication. GFC saw IT—in particular its satellite system and the Internet—as key tools for increasing communication and learning within the firm.

Because GFC will continue to use its current software as well as develop new applications to support collaborative work and sharing of information, the two streams of literature of particular relevance to this case are CSCW (Computer Supported Cooperative Work) and CMC (Computer-Mediated Communication). CSCW and CMC are two broad and overlapping interdisciplinary fields with participants from software design, human-computer interaction, management, and sociology. In general, CSCW focuses more on software applications (often called "groupware") that allow colleagues who are not physically located in the same place to share information, communicate, and collaborate. CMC usually refers to person-to-person communication using computer networks and tends to look more at the social and organizational issues involved in how people work and communicate with each other. Both fields are based on the understanding that most work is carried out in a social context, and both tend to put a rather positive spin on the prospect of collaboration.

Although e-mail is the most common application studied by CSCW researchers, more effort has recently gone into developing and studying applications such as coauthoring tools, intelligent databases, and group-decision support systems. The main purpose of these shared databases is to gain information and expertise from colleagues who may not be available locally, and to establish and maintain interpersonal social ties, particularly so-called "weak ties."[28] There are two fundamentally different approaches to developing knowledge-sharing databases or digital libraries to which employees contribute. One approach is to enter the individuals' knowledge into the database and develop new ways of searching the data. The second is to enable searching of meta-data about individuals who possess the information that someone might need. One seeks to eliminate the need for individuals; the other seeks to bring people together so that they can learn from each other. Though databases and other CSCW software are often seen as a panacea to communication problems in an organization, getting people to share information is rarely easy or straightforward. For example, Constant, Sproull, and Kiesler (1999: 415) found that people in organizations prefer to exchange help with those who are in close proximity, are part of a group membership, have a history of prior relationships, and share demographic similarities. They were more reluctant to depend on unknown colleagues at distant locations for technical advice—depending on the kindness of strangers—because they had no way of assessing the reliability, knowledge, or motive of the provider. In addition, Grudin (1990) notes that the software can bring unequal benefits to those who use the application, lead to activity that violates social taboos, threaten existing political structures, and demotivate users. Groupware can also be inflexible, and its development, in spite of its name, is often based on supporting single users rather than groups.

Computer Supported Cooperative Work and Computer-Mediated Communication overlap a great deal, but where CSCW focuses on the development of collaborative software, CMC concentrates more on the act of communication between people and is not as goal- or task-driven. Though CMC can be very broadly defined, some authors such as Pickering and King (1995: 479–480) define it as person-to-person communication, often in text or graphic form, over computer networks, with e-mail as the most common example. As they note, these technologies have long been expected to bring serious challenges to organizational hierarchy by encouraging more democratic communication, but in spite of the rhetoric surrounding their transformational power, there is little evidence that these changes occur. For example, a common statement is that CMC is inherently democratic because the focus is on individuals' ideas, not their appearance, gender, age, race, body shape, hair color, or clothes, and therefore permits low-status or marginalized individuals to participate more freely. The findings have been mixed, however. Some studies have concluded that e-mail and similar applications do reduce the importance of cues such as age, status, gender, and race, and therefore the messages (and the respective individual authors) are recognized or distinguished by the content of their ideas.[29] Other work is not so optimistic. For example, Susan Herring (1996) writes that contrary to the belief that the technology allows women to participate, female academics face the same problems online as they do in their own institutions. She says that "despite the democratizing potential . . . male and female academic professionals do not participate equally in academic CMC. Rather, a small male minority dominates the discourse both in terms of amount of talk, and rhetorically, through self-promotional and adversarial strategies. Moreover, when women do attempt to participate on a more equal basis, they risk being actively censored by the reactions of men who either ignore them or attempt to delegitimize their contributions. Because of social conditioning that makes women uncomfortable with direct conflict, women tend to be more intimidated by these practices and to avoid participating as a result. . . . [The] conditions for a democratic discourse are not met: although the medium theoretically allows for everyone with access to a network to take part and to express their concerns and desires equally, a very large community of potential participants is effectively prevented by censorship, both overt and covert, from availing itself of this possibility. Rather than being democratic, academic CMC is power-based and hierarchical. This state of affairs cannot, however, be attributed to the influence of computer communication technology; rather it continues preexisting patterns of hierarchy and male dominance in academia more generally, and in society as a whole" (1996: 486).

In any case, both sets of literature highlight the challenges that GFC will face when developing software and tools to encourage collaboration, sharing of knowledge, and communication within the workplace. The simple lesson here is that information technology is not a panacea, it is not magic, and

GFC will not be able to rely on a piece of software or technology to make fundamental organizational changes in their firm or to alter strongly held positions of their employees.

COMMUNICATION BETWEEN DEALERSHIPS AND THE MANUFACTURER

There is a constant and extensive flow of communication and information between the manufacturer in Detroit and the dealerships, but the direction tends to be one-way and top-down. Communication consists primarily of the daily satellite training broadcasts, regular visits from the regional staff, and a box of printed material delivered weekly to every dealership.

The DES training gathers feedback from all employees and acts as both a collector and distributor of best practices. As one host said, "If you're doing something cool, I'd love to hear about it. If there's something driving you crazy, bring it up." However, few participants take advantage of this communication channel, in large part because getting through to the program host can be so difficult. Shared experience seems to be better communicated when it is incorporated into the training broadcast itself. For example, it is not uncommon for the broadcast to feature a dealership or several dealerships that are taking a different approach to a problem. The videos describe the new practice with enough detail to make it credible to dealers. In addition, it is shown as an alternative approach that has worked for some dealerships, not the one and only answer. The dealership employees explain why they tried this solution and the results they have had. This works well because dealers are typically wary about trying out new techniques suggested by the managers in Detroit, but seeing and hearing about the experience from other dealers who work in similar conditions is reassuring and more credible, making it easier for each dealership to decide if the practice might be right for it.

Another form of communication is via the regional field staff who regularly visit each dealership every two to four weeks and who are employees of the manufacturer. One of their roles is to encourage dealerships to participate in incentive programs. A field staff person jokingly said that his job was to pester and nag the dealerships to sell more. But more important, field staff can also act as conduits between Detroit and the dealers. Not only does the regional representative provide a personal face to the manufacturer with whom the dealers can interact and present their case, but problems or difficulties that dealers are facing can much more easily be transferred up the chain of command. Good field representatives can reduce the distance between the head office and the dealerships, and in this way can make a very large corporation seem more accessible. Dealers can argue and explain why they object to a policy or program, and the field rep can explain the reasoning behind the decision. Because the field staff are responsible for a dozen dealers in the region, they will also have the ability to judge whether a dealer's objections are limited to that one store or if they are shared more widely. And because they usually have extensive experience in the business, they are often able to decide whether the complaint or objection is legitimate. If it is, and if many dealers share it, the field representative can bring the concern to the attention of the head office.

Also at the regional field office are the staff in the customer service department, who mediate any dispute between customers and dealers. Their role is important because even though warranty policies are relatively straightforward, the repair problems are rarely simple or clear-cut, and customers often do not read or understand their policy. A sympathetic customer service representative at the regional level can be a godsend to the service manager because repairs that are not covered under the warranty have to be paid for by either the dealership or the customer. If the customer refuses to pay for a repair for any reason, the dealership is obliged to cover the cost, not the manufacturer. The customer service rep has the ability to bend the manufacturer's rules and under certain circumstances extend the customer's warranty to cover the cost of the repair for service managers whom they trust and know have made good faith efforts to resolve the problem themselves.

For example, in one GFC dealership a customer brought in his car for a recall on a part. Usually the technician will do a short test drive before working on a car, but the vehicle was brought in with an empty fuel tank so the technician just replaced the part. The customer picked up the vehicle and complained that now it was making a thumping noise at the rear (the replaced part was at the front) and accused the dealership of damaging his car. Indeed, there was a serious problem in the rear, but the problem was preexisting and had nothing to do with the replaced part. The dealership did not want to pay and the customer refused. The service manager called up the customer support rep and explained the problem. He admitted that it was their own fault—the technician should have put gas in the car and checked it out first, as is their policy, but he had not because it had been such a hectic day. Because the customer support representative knew the manager and the dealership had a good reputation, he gave permission for the dealership to fix the new problem and have the warranty cover the cost.

In addition to training broadcasts and personal interaction with regional representatives, dealerships regularly receive large quantities of print material. GFC sends a large box every week containing information on parts, recalls, service, and sales, as well as general information for owners, dealers, and managers. The material is separated into packets for each department. The main complaint on the part of the dealers is the sheer volume of information (managers are so busy, they do not have time to go through it carefully), and the system can occasionally break down if the person distributing the packets delivers it to the wrong individual or destination. Most manufacturers, including GFC, have plans to or already distribute this information via the Internet, which would certainly reduce printing and shipping costs and make the information more accessible, but still would not address the problem of employees lacking the time to read the information.

In spite of the rather extensive flow of information from the manufacturer to the dealerships, dealers often complain that they are often left in the dark on some of the most important issues, whether it is plans for a major organizational restructuring or information on vehicle recalls.[30]

The flow of information between Detroit and the dealerships is not all top-down however. There are some mechanisms that allow dealership employees to communicate with the GFC head office. Technicians probably have the most options. The manufacturers all have somewhat different systems, but GFC, for example, has an electronic reporting system that was established to identify vehicle problems in a timely manner. Technicians in the field who identify a problem or potential problem are supposed to inform service engineers in Detroit, who begin to develop an appropriate repair procedure, which would then be made available to all technicians. The system, however, is generally considered to be slow, complicated, and awkward. It was also set up to capture the experience of the most experienced technicians, but in many shops it is the hourly and least experienced technicians who use it the most. One service manager speculated that the inexperienced technicians used it to make themselves feel important. In contrast, the highly skilled and experienced technicians who theoretically would have the most valuable information to contribute tended to see it as a waste of time, simply because either it was too much bother or they were paid by the job rather than the hour and therefore had no financial incentive to participate.

There are also formal administrative committees created to encourage the flow of information from the dealerships to the manufacturer. For example, GFC parts managers have a formal committee that represents them and presents their concerns to the head office. An individual can submit a suggestion to the committee, which moves it up to the manufacturer. In the eyes of parts managers, this has been quite successful because it diminishes the sense that the individual would be David in a battle with Goliath. Having the suggestion go through the committee not only depersonalizes it, but also adds legitimacy, given that fellow members must agree with the suggestion or complaint in order for it to move up the communication chain.

COMMUNICATION BETWEEN DEALERSHIPS

Because all dealerships are in competition with each other, even those with the same manufacturer, it is not surprising to find that there is not a high level of communication and contact between them. But there is certainly some, and dealers and managers seem to welcome and enjoy the opportunity to socialize and talk about their work. Clearly they have a great deal in common, but the nature of their business forces them to remain at arm's length.[31]

The manufacturer will often organize special meetings and seminars for dealers and managers that help to bridge the communication gap between dealerships. There are also regional clubs for service and parts managers that meet monthly. Not all managers attend these meetings, however, because they are so busy, and many find it difficult to leave work for an entire afternoon. And, understandably, many are not enthused about attending meetings outside of work hours when their days are already so long. In a few cases, managers say that their dealers discourage them from attending. These clubs are often seen very positively by their members because it is their sole opportunity to talk with others in the same field and learn from each other. And though these groups have been quite vociferous in their criticism of the head office in the past, which clearly did not please the man-ufacturer, apparently the climate is beginning to change, as the head office is becoming much more willing to listen.

The Distance Education System is another mechanism for communica-tion and learning from other dealerships, albeit with the Detroit office act-ing as mediator. It is a more or less useful way of sharing experiences and helping dealership employees understand that they are part of a wider pro-fessional community.

Locally, the greatest amount of direct and regular cooperation and shar-ing of resources happens between the individual parts departments of GFC dealerships. If a dealership urgently needs a part that is not in stock, the parts employee will check the inventory of all the local GFC dealerships and contact the nearest one to find it. If the part is available, the dealership will usually sell it at cost, knowing that the favor will be reciprocated one day in the future.

COMMUNICATION BETWEEN EMPLOYEES

The amount of communication, sense of community, and sharing of knowledge between employees in the dealership depend on the employees' positions.

For the technicians, the physical environment is not particularly con-ducive to sharing information. The shop is usually noisy, and the service bays are usually too far apart for easy conversation. But in addition to coffee and lunch breaks, technicians do have ways to socialize and talk about prob-lems they are having with a particularly difficult repair job. Depending on the individual and how the shop is arranged, discussion can happen in the dispatcher's office. This is particularly true if the technicians have a reason to be in the office other than to drop off or pick up work orders. One dis-patcher intentionally put the shop's technical information system in his of-fice so that he could informally monitor how the technicians' jobs were pro-gressing, and so they could discuss the repair with him or other technicians if they were having problems. Waiting to pick up parts at the parts counter is another common way to converse with fellow workers.

Because the sales staff tend to be gregarious people, they go out of their way to talk, and their work environment allows them to do so. The show-room is relatively quiet, pleasant, and conducive to conversation. Salespeople have desks assigned to them, but when they are not on the phone, doing paperwork, or with a customer, they tend to cluster together in a common area, often near the sales manager's desk or by the coffee machine. Their talk is usually light, revolving around sports, cars, weather, restaurants, news stories, travel plans, or television shows, but work issues are sometimes discussed. Difficult customer stories are popular. Though they enjoy talking, they are reluctant to share knowledge and experience because they are in active competition with each other for customers.

In contrast, though the parts counter employees talk and share information with each other a great deal, it is the service advisors who are the real communicators in any dealership. Not only do they work within a few feet of each other, but much of their work is verbal, which means that they can easily overhear what the others are saying. Talking between service advisors seems to be important for the smooth functioning of the service desk because they often have to cover for a colleague or pick up some of their work temporarily. Having colleagues who are knowledgeable and competent is a boon because it means they can be depended on to fill in (and not make mistakes) if the other is called away from their desk, whether it be for a meeting, a discussion with a technician, or an emergency at home. Because they receive so little formal training, they depend on their colleagues to teach them. Joking and teasing also seem to act as an important pressure valve for them, helping to relieve the stress of the job. Some of the chat is personal (they talk about their kids, a television program they all watched, politics, and their plans for the weekend), but much is also work-related. They remind each other about the correct way to handle a problem, and there is much over-the-shoulder help, assistance, informal monitoring, and comments from their colleagues if they have doubts or questions about a situation.

The Individual

SALESPEOPLE

Salespeople come from all walks of life. Many come with some type of sales experience, but it is not unusual for them to have held jobs such as medical technician, insurance salesman, engineer, accountant, gas station manager, restaurateur, or musician.

One sales manager explained that many people end up in automobile sales "by accident or necessity," meaning that few seek it as their first career choice. Another manager said, "It's one business where you don't need a resumé," and still another called his staff a "rogue's gallery." Few people enter automobile sales right out of school, and when asked why it is not more popular as a career choice, salespeople usually describe car sales as a retail business with long hours and a long workweek. Others suggest that the negative stereotype of the car salesman has a negative impact on recruitment to the ranks. In 1973, Robert Throckmorton wrote that the auto salesman occupies an unenviable position in our society. On one hand, the auto salesman can be seen as a strategic member of an occupation that is crucial for the existence of our society. On the other he is seen as the member of an occupation held in extreme low esteem. Auto sales is viewed as an occupation that is a "waste of a college education, no job for a man with talent and brains," whose membership consists of persons generally seen as "arrogant, liars, cheats, crooks" and "cigar-chewing, sloppily-dressed, dishonest drifters" (42–43). Spinella et al. added, "People seek them out at social events, but don't necessarily want their daughters to marry one" (1978: 11). In any case, it is not exactly a reputation that would inspire young people to join the profession.

Sales is a tough job, but just how tough is a matter of opinion. One view sees it as brutal and extremely stressful. (Of course, attached to this is a certain amount of pride in having not only survived but thrived in such a difficult environment.) This group sees sales as a far more difficult working environment than the service department. One salesman compared the position to being a caveman, who has to go out every day and hunt the meat he and his family are going to eat. To succeed in sales, he suggested, a person has to be "hungry," be aggressive (but not so aggressive that you alienate customers), have stamina, be a workaholic, be independent, and be willing to work Sundays and nights and miss your kids' birthdays. In short, you have to be driven because it's a "dog-eat-dog" job with a high stress level. The other view is a little less extreme. Sales reps from this group tend to think that they work in a somewhat more kinder and gentler place and consider their job to be at least calmer, if not easier, than what the service advisors and managers have to face every day.

So why take a job as an automobile salesperson? What is the reward for such apparent difficulty and stress? The answer is, primarily, the possibility of earning a lot of money. In addition, a position in sales is the fastest route to a general manager's job or even to becoming a dealer (NADA 1973). But when pressed, many will admit that it is more than just making money. As one salesman acknowledged, there is "the thrill of getting someone to spend a lot of money because of something I said." Over and above the monthly paycheck, they find pleasure, power, and a thrill in selling.

There is a long laundry list of important qualities that successful automobile salespeople share. One of the most important, not surprisingly, is people skills: the ability to listen, a "good" personality, and the ability to make people feel comfortable. This ability to break down barriers is important because customers often come in feeling wary either because they have had a bad experience elsewhere or because they are expecting the stereotypical salesman. As one salesperson said, "You have to convince your customer that you're human, too." And then, once the customer is comfortable, you need to "obligate" them, meaning that after you show them the cars, take them on a demonstration drive, and generally win them over with your personality, you want them to feel obligated to buy from you.

Salespeople have to be calm and sincere as well as flexible and adaptable because they have to deal with a wide variety of customers. They have to be relatively intelligent, able to communicate well, inoffensive in their manner, easy to understand, upbeat, and respectful, and have a good attitude. One salesperson summarized it thus: to sell cars you need to treat people right, be nice, be fair, and be nice to the people you work with.[32]

Car salespeople must have, or at least appear to have, a genuine liking for people. Joy Browne in *The Used-Car Game* (1973: 19–20) makes the point that most people assume that the salesperson's friendliness is feigned, but it is not. When there are customers, "things really move. It's exciting and lively and unpredictable and challenging and, as they admit, just plain fun. When no customers are around, their existence is unimaginably boring. There is nothing to do and nobody to see and all the time in the world to do it in. . . . So, part of the eagerness and friendliness with which the salesman greets the customer isn't feigned at all. In addition to having a sales prospect, he's very glad to have someone to talk to."

Though the liking for people may be genuine, salespeople will always say that acting ability is a necessity for success. As one sales rep explained, if a blue-collar worker comes in looking for a car, you have to become like that person. If a Harvard MBA walks in, you have to become one of them. You have to change your personality to match the customer—a technique they call "reading the customer" or "mirror and match." The very best salespeople, according to sales reps, possess a chameleon-like ability—they can become anyone, and they manage to do so with convincing sincerity. It makes sense to make the customer as comfortable as possible, but from a consumer's point of view this ability has a negative connotation. As one salesman explained, customers have to like you if they're going to buy a car from you, but you can't be a "nice guy" if you're going to make money, so you have to convince the customer that you are, without necessarily being one.[33]

Good sales reps also claim to possess an intuition about people, or an ability to "read" customers. For example, some salespeople claim that they can tell if a person is serious about buying a car simply by how the customer looks as he or she walks in the door. This belief in the ability to understand customers by looking at their physical characteristics and mannerisms actually dates back to the earliest days of automobile sales. In 1923, Ford published a series of manuals for its sales force training called *Ford Products and Their Sale*, which had a section titled "How to Read Human Nature and Fit Your Selling Talk to the Man." In it was a section called "Proportionate Shape of Head," which described the different approaches a salesman should take depending on the shape and height of the customer's forehead. A high head was supposed to indicate an idealistic person; a medium head was thought to be more commercially minded; and a low head indicated that the customer could be reached through a sense of the physical (Tedlow 1990: 157). Understanding the customer's character via physical traits was intended to help the salesmen alter their sales pitch to suit the customer's type, and therefore sell more effectively.

Tenacity, in-depth knowledge of the product, and the ability to work independently are also highly valued qualities, because sales reps have to constantly follow up with clients who come in to look but do not buy. Good salespeople will follow up and call customers as often as necessary to make a sale. They call customers who have purchased a car and ask them how things are going, they send birthday cards, and they call out of the blue to ask if an owner is interested in trading-in and buying a new car. The purpose is "to keep your name in the customer's head," because the amount of follow-up that salespeople do is directly proportional to sales, which in turn is directly proportional to their income.

Though it is easy to describe a good salesperson, it is not always easy for dealers to identify people with those qualities, and they are the first to admit that they are often surprised by who succeeds and who does not. But in general, sales managers know within a couple of months if a new employee is cut out to be a salesperson. In a curious twist, unlike with most other jobs, more experience does not necessarily translate into higher sales or better performance. Some salespeople who perform well initially can sell fewer cars over time because they start to take shortcuts in their sales technique. Managers tell stories of sales reps who go from selling twelve to fourteen cars a month down to four. Success in sales, it seems, all comes down to a rather mysterious personal quality that one either has or hasn't, combined with good technique.

Turnover is high, and most new salespeople do not make it past the first year. One sales manager's rule-of-thumb is that out of ten people who come in without an automotive background, nine will quit within the first twelve months. To reduce the turnover, many dealerships are now making an effort to be more selective in their hiring practices. Sales managers also find that they have to be a little more tolerant of a less-than-stellar sales record. In the past they would just let weak performers go, but now they tend to focus on those underperformers, working on their weaknesses and building on their strengths. Sales managers claim that the days of using the Darwinian method of hiring large numbers of inexperienced and untrained salespeople and then letting most of them fail are almost over.

SERVICE ADVISORS

Service advisors, who are also called "technical writers" or "service writers," come from a wide variety of backgrounds. Many have automobile or dealership experience of some kind, but it is not a prerequisite. In fact, some suggest that *not* having a technical background is actually an asset because it means that they are less likely to try to diagnose the vehicle's problem—a diagnosis that could mislead or confuse the customer. The service advisor's primary job is to listen to the customer and to record and describe the problem, not to diagnose or second-guess the technician.

Some knowledge about automotive repair and the basic operation of a car is obviously an advantage, but if a service advisor does not start with that expertise, he or she will usually gain it on the job. For a service advisor, people skills, not technical expertise, are by far the most important. The best advisors are polite, upbeat, knowledgeable, patient, and helpful. Because they are often the ones who deliver bad news to the customers, they need to be tactful, professional, and empathetic. And because they bear the brunt of the customer's frustration, they need to be not so much thick-skinned as able to avoid taking the customer's anger personally.

PARTS EMPLOYEES

Most parts employees have either an automotive background or dealership experience. They usually learn the job slowly by working their way up through the ranks, for example, from driver on the lot, to warranty, to receiving, and eventually to the parts counter.

The staff at the parts counter require the same people skills as the service advisors, even though they usually deal with the dealership technicians rather than the public. They bear the brunt of the technicians' frustrations—technicians can be as argumentative, demanding, impatient, and difficult as the public—and like the service advisors, the parts employees must learn that criticism is not to be taken too personally. Parts department staff need negotiating skills, patience, and good technical knowledge because they often discuss the choice of parts with technicians. They need to be detail-oriented and, above all, have an incredible memory for numbers.

TECHNICIANS

Technicians usually became involved in the automotive field while growing up, and most who enter the business today earn a formal automotive training program degree after completing high school. But because automotive technology is rapidly becoming more complex, manufacturers are requiring more formal and on-the-job training for the technicians. As the U.S. Department of Labor states, "There are more computers aboard a car today than aboard the first spaceship" (Kirby 1998: 2). As a result, knowledge of electronics has become increasingly important. In addition to computer skills, strong communication, analytical, and mathematical skills are required to keep abreast of the new technology.[34]

But any technician or service manager will tell you that probably the most important quality a technician needs is a love of cars. Most good technicians will say that cars have always fascinated them and that they grew up tinkering with cars in a garage. The best technicians are always described as having a "knack" for diagnosing problems. Service managers claim that just because a person is a certified mechanic and scores well on all the tests does not necessarily mean that he can fix cars—he needs to have a talent for identifying and repairing the problem. This knack or intuitive feel is also the attribute in which technicians take the most pride. As a retired technical trainer said, the best technician "is a guy who can put his hand on the [engine] hood and tell you the third cylinder is missing."

Technicians work at a dealership five or more years on average, but some stay for twelve to twenty years. The turnover is fairly low, but when technicians do move to a new job, they will usually stay with the same line or manufacturer of vehicle. Any good technician, in theory, could learn to repair any make of vehicle, but they would have to start again at the beginning and learn the idiosyncrasies of the new line, which would slow them down and reduce their pay—something that few technicians are willing to do. Because good technicians are few and far between, dealers are making a greater effort to keep them by paying good salaries and creating a better work environment. In the past, experienced technicians migrated from the shop to the front office (administrative positions) in their careers, but this rarely happens anymore because they can make more money repairing vehicles than they can in management.

In any shop there is usually a mix of skilled technicians and "hourly guys," employees paid by the hour for routine maintenance work. Technicians are graded and certified. The most highly skilled and experienced technicians will usually have a specialty such as transmissions, air-conditioning, front-end, or brakes, while technicians with less training and experience will perform tune-ups by adjusting the ignition timing and valves, or adjusting or replacing spark plugs or other parts to ensure efficient engine performance (Bureau of Labor Statistics 2007).

Cultural and Social Environment

Workplace culture, though less visible and infrequently acknowledged, can have a profound impact on how or if employees communicate and learn, and is intrinsically tied to how customers and employees are treated. In this area, GFC faces major obstacles.

RELATIONSHIP BETWEEN HEAD OFFICE

AND DEALERSHIP EMPLOYEES

One of the primary obstacles to open communication is the fear of reprisal. Many dealers are concerned that if they appear to be critical, the head office will retaliate. Clearly the most extreme punishment would be to revoke the franchise agreement, but there are many other ways to punish a dealership. Customer field representatives might not be so accommodating with warranty disputes, deliveries could be delayed, the most popular and desirable vehicles might not be as readily available, or the manufacturer could request an audit.[35]

Regrettably, many dealers manage to reproduce the same climate of fear within their own businesses. An atmosphere of distrust and wariness permeates the workplace, and as a result employees hesitate to suggest new ideas or volunteer any information. Employees feel that their ideas are not listened to, or they believe that honest opinions can only serve to get them in trouble with the owner or their supervisors. There is a sense that the less communication there is, the safer they are.[36]

Employees' reluctance to share their experience or make suggestions is reinforced when their ideas are ignored or rejected. Manufacturers know that their technicians possess extremely useful information, and most have developed a variety of ways to tap into that experience. However, for any system to work, not only do technicians need to send the information, but someone needs to receive and act on that information. Apparently the college-educated engineers at the head office are often not enthusiastic recipients of the technicians' suggestions, for two reasons. First, they tend to dismiss contributions or suggestions made by the technicians because they view them as mere high school dropouts with little to offer.[37] Second, the product design process itself poses a problem because the engineers view the issues and solutions that the technicians bring up as "old" problems of "old" products. Even late models are considered "old" because the engineering department primary focuses on current and future models. In contrast, the service department faces older models on a daily basis. Their workday is spent repairing the models that the Detroit engineers have long since forgotten or ceased to care about.

There is also the more human problem of people simply not wanting to admit that they are wrong or not wanting to acknowledge that someone else is right. A story about a problem with a car alarm system illustrates this well. A new SUV was brought into the shop by a customer because the anti-theft alarm could not be "armed." The dealership technicians then discovered the same problem with two other new vehicles on the lot. The technician went through the usual problem-solving processes, consulted all the manuals and technical bulletins, and used all the available diagnostic tools, which only indicated that the system was working fine. The technician called the head office as well as the factory where the vehicle was made, but neither source was able to solve the mystery. The technician started to dismantle the system to see if he could identify the problem visually. Eventually he found it. A short piece of wire, not listed in the manual, was establishing a circuit between two junction blocks, which was shorting out the system, making the alarm unable to detect if the doors were locked. Simply cutting the piece of wire broke the circuit, and the problem was fixed. This technician had spent a great deal of time and energy fixing this problem and understandably was pleased with his success. He then wrote up a report, describing the problem and how he solved it, and sent it in to the manufacturer. Normally, technicians who find fixes to known problems receive a cash reward, and this technician expected to receive some type of recognition for his detective work. He then heard that he would not receive anything because in the manufacturer's eyes this had not been a "technical" problem that needed to be solved. As it turned out, when customers order this type of SUV, they have the option of declining the security system and receiving a credit of $270. But because it is too complicated to build some vehicles with an alarm system and some without, the factory built all of them with an alarm system, and if the customer declined that option, the factory would short the system on that vehicle. The problem in this case had been an order mix-up. The dealership had ordered three vehicles with an alarm system and the factory thought they had requested vehicles without them. The technician had solved what was clearly a problem to him and the customer, but to the head office it was an administrative problem that had nothing to do with the technician. Though they eventually relented, initially the manufacturer dismissed the technician's efforts as irrelevant and had no intention of compensating him or recognizing his work.

Unfortunately, this type of event happens from time to time in any workplace, but the repercussions are very serious because that one event can become symbolic of how seriously the head office takes the technicians and their expertise. Next time, not only will that particular technician not bother to share his experience and discoveries with the head office, but it is very likely that everyone else in that shop who has heard of the injustice will be reluctant as well. By choosing to define the problem so narrowly and dismissing the technician's obvious diligence, persistence, and problem-solving skills, the manufacturer lost the goodwill and future best practices of all the technicians in that shop for several years.

This story illustrates how problems are very much in the eye of the beholder. To the manufacturer, it was an administrative problem. To the technician, it was a technical problem, and to the dealer and the customer it was a financial problem. Because one person's "problem" is often another person's "mistake," it is not surprising that individuals redefine problems to make their mistakes more acceptable or to shift blame. It also points to one of the main challenges of creating organizational databases of shared practices. Though organizations and individuals can and do learn from their mistakes, it is a rare employee or department that is willing to publicly admit their mistakes and embed them in their organization's community memory.

The literature on organizational learning and communication emphasizes that employees will only share information if (1) it is easy to find out who specifically in the organization needs the information; and (2) it is easy to contact this person (Huber 1996; Lipshitz et al. 1996). This is inarguably true, but it implies that sharing knowledge is a mechanical process and all that managers need is to provide an open pipeline and the shared knowledge will automatically flow. The security alarm story, however, illustrates that sharing information is more subtle and complex than just knowing who needs the information and having a way of getting that information to the proper person. The story also highlights how managers must be extremely sensitive to how they encourage and motivate people to share their experience and to just how little it takes to discourage employees from participating.

The goal of encouraging communication and building a community of practice between local dealerships is also complicated by the ever-present sense of competition and distrust between dealers—after all, the "other guy" could easily steal their customers or employees if they are not careful. Under these conditions any hope of creating a community would appear to be rather slight, but some interesting research has been done by Andreas Pyka

(1997) and Stephan Schrader (1992) that suggests otherwise. Their work demonstrated that the sharing of information can and does occur between colleagues in different firms, even firms that are in active competition. This may at first seem counterintuitive, given that we usually assume firms wish to keep their collective knowledge a secret in order to gain a competitive advantage. But Pyka's research (1997: 217) shows that firms and individuals often *deliberately* leak and share knowledge with others, and that informal networking is an important mechanism for information diffusion. In fact, Schrader (1992: 320–327) found that employees frequently exchange proprietary information with colleagues in other firms, including direct competitors, in the expectation of receiving valuable information in return.[38]

CUSTOMER RELATIONS

The changing customer has presented automobile dealerships with some of their biggest challenges. Customers are no longer loyal to a certain make, and they are more knowledgeable and demanding. The demographics have shifted as well, with more women having either a significant or final say in the purchase of a vehicle, and many having the sole responsibility for servicing their vehicles. For the first time in their history, dealerships can no longer flourish simply by waiting for the customers to come to them. Dealers now have to work much harder to get and keep customers, sales reps are urged to be less aggressive and more respectful of customers, and the service department tries to be more user-friendly.

The manufacturers now encourage "relationship marketing," which emphasizes increasing customer loyalty, creating stronger ties with customers, and ultimately encouraging customers to stay with the same dealership for all their sales, repair, and maintenance needs.[39] Even though a greater focus on respect for the customer does not seem to be a particularly new or groundbreaking idea, for dealerships it has been a monumental shift, and the transition has not always been easy. It is on the showroom floor and at the service counter where management theory and new marketing strategies clash with human egos and self-image. While there may be a greater emphasis placed on customer satisfaction, the relationship between customers and the dealership continues to be strained because of old habits, attitudes, and stereotypes.

From the customer's perspective, going to an automobile dealership for service or to buy a new car is rarely an enjoyable experience. They distrust the salespeople and suspect that they will be taken advantage of whenever possible. For women, automobile dealerships are notoriously unpleasant. In the service department, the expectations are equally negative because customers tend to go to dealerships only when something is wrong with their car, the experience almost always involves paying a lot of money, and making the effort to get there and arrange for alternate transportation is inconvenient and disruptive to their daily routine. In addition, they may feel inadequate if they do not understand auto mechanics, what is expected of them, or the vocabulary of cars and car repair. Dealerships add to the uncertainty and confusion with inadequate signage and difficult-to-understand bills. Not surprisingly, the result is often a distrustful, suspicious, frustrated, and unhappy customer.

Overcoming the problems of vulnerability and trust is extremely difficult. Customers arrive feeling vulnerable, especially when they lack information, expertise, freedom to go elsewhere, or recourse if things go wrong (Seiders and Berry 1998). There also may be a gap between the expectations of the customer and those of the management that can cause problems and misunderstandings (Parasuraman, Berry, and Zeithaml 1991). An example of the frustration that a customer can experience and how things can so easily go wrong was demonstrated one day at a dealership. In the waiting room (it was in a temporary portable room because the dealership was being renovated) a customer was furious because he had been waiting for over three hours. He had arrived on time for his appointment and handed over his keys and vehicle to the "greeter," to whom he explained the reason for his visit—a simple maintenance task. He received a tag and went to the waiting room. Unfortunately, the customer had never been to the dealership before, and the greeter had not informed him that he still needed to check in with the service advisors. Two hours later, after becoming more and more angry, the customer finally confronted a staff member. The staff member discovered that the service advisors had the keys but had not bothered to find out who owned them, and so the job had not even begun. The people at the service desk were less than sympathetic because from their perspective, the customer had "missed" his appointment and therefore was in the wrong, but they grudgingly agreed to reschedule for later that morning, and the work was eventually done. A simple thirty-minute maintenance job had turned into a four-hour ordeal, both parties were angry, and both blamed each other for the problem.

The problem of trust is particularly acute in auto dealerships because of three typical characteristics: (1) the transaction often involves a large sum of money; (2) the customer and the dealership employee know that the transaction is zero-sum: the less the customer pays, the less profit the dealership makes; and (3) the transaction contains a serious information imbalance. This is especially true in the service department, where the technician and the service advisor know much more than the customer about the true nature of the problem, the repairs that are required (as opposed to desirable), the dealer's actual cost for labor and repairs, and so on. Almost every transaction has one or two of these characteristics, but the combination of all three can lead to substantial customer anxiety.

On the other side, dealership staff maintain an almost equally dark view of customers. Customers are seen as demanding, difficult, uncooperative, and generally unreasonable people who argue over normal prices and refuse to accept reasonable explanations. From the dealership's perspective, customers create problems and generally make life difficult for them. The unhappy result is that the relationship between customers and dealership staff is often adversarial, and because both parties tend to see the other as threatening, the result all too frequently is a tense standoff and a lack of communication.

Obviously there are some customers who are completely unreasonable and there are some dealership employees who are unethical, but in this relationship the worst case scenario—the most unreasonable customer and the most underhanded dealership employee—is assumed to be the norm rather the exception. Under these circumstances it takes enormous effort and a great deal of charm and empathy on both sides to break through the negative stereotypes.

The Internet has also been responsible for a major power shift between customers and dealerships, and has shaken the sales department to the core. Buying a car in the past was an intimidating and traumatic experience for most consumers because they would arrive in a showroom without knowing much at all about the vehicles they were looking at, and knowing even less about the sales process. On top of their unfamiliarity, customers often had to face the sales team's heavy pressure and strong-arm sales tactics, all of which added up to a less-than-satisfactory experience for the consumer.

The Internet, as well as other print sources, has drastically shifted this imbalance of knowledge, with consumers now enjoying access to a wide range of advice, reviews, reports, specifications, pricing data, invoice pricing, information on dealer holdbacks, and factory incentives—all details that were once privileged information. A recent J.D. Powers New Autoshopper.com Study reported that 49 percent of new vehicle buyers claim that the Internet influenced their choice of make, model, and price they were willing to pay (Ward's Dealer Business 2003). Because of the widely accessible consumer information on the Internet, customers have become more knowledgeable and discriminating, all of which contributes to a lower markup (and profit) on vehicle sales. But there is a bright side from the seller's perspective. While dealers may justifiably blame their shrinking profits on increasing consumer knowledge, that information also makes consumers more comfortable with the sales process, which can make it easier for the salesperson to close a deal.

For the salespeople, the reduced profit on each vehicle has had repercussions on their work, but even more profound has been the change in their customers. Customers are different today: they are more knowledgeable, more demanding, do not buy impulsively, and are a tougher sell in general. Customers expect politeness, respect, and consideration and are willing to go elsewhere if they do not get it. Gone are the days when the more aggressive salesmen talked about "putting the customer to sleep" (that is, numbing and overwhelming them with talk). That technique no longer works. As one salesman said, "You have to kill them with kindness, be tenacious over the phone, and give them a good price." Salespeople regret that customers no longer walk into the showroom and buy a car. On average it takes about two to four weeks for a customer to select and buy a car, and if everything works normally, a sales rep will spend about two to three hours of contact time with the customer (face-to-face or by telephone) spread over that period.

Salespeople are also now expected to sell to a whole new group of consumers—women—which has not been easy or smooth. It would be a gross understatement to say that the automobile business has largely been a male-oriented culture. For most of its history, the automobile industry has either ignored women or not taken them seriously, either as consumers or employees. As Sanford (1983: 137) noted, the literature on the automobile "clearly leaves women's voices in the back seat," and anyone who addresses women in this context is "almost lost in an all-male chorus up front." The 1948 drawing in Figure 4.3 illustrates the traditional attitude toward women as consumers at the time—they were expected to sit quietly reading a magazine while the man discussed the financial details with the salesman.

Figure 4.3. 1948 sales office
SOURCE: General Motors Corporation 1948: 20.

Though it may make obvious and excellent business sense to start paying attention to a forgotten half of the population, it has not been an easy transition for automobile dealerships. Manufacturers have had to introduce training programs that focus on selling to women, trying to break down the stereotype that salesmen typically have about women by emphasizing that many women work, earn good salaries, and buy cars. Even when they are not the primary buyer, women have tremendous influence over the final purchase decision. The message that the manufacturers push is that women are important potential customers and salespeople ignore them at their financial peril.

There are still very few women working in dealerships except in clerical or sometimes service advisor positions, and many salesmen still tend to subtly (or not so subtly) ignore or act in a condescending manner toward female customers. One female salesperson acknowledged that she had been treated badly when she went to purchase a vehicle in the past. She saw that even in her own dealership women were treated more disrespectfully than men, and as a result, intended to offer a class at her church to teach women how to fight back and avoid being taken advantage of by salesmen.

Also noteworthy is the nonrelationship between technicians and customers. Though good technicians are highly valued, most dealers try to keep technicians and customers apart. Unlike in a small independent repair shop, where a technician would likely have the opportunity to discuss the vehicle directly with the owner, dealership technicians are often isolated from the customer. This is done because, according to one manager, though the technicians may be very good at repairing vehicles, their "social skills" may be wanting. Service managers fear that technicians either could alienate customers by being curt, impolite, or rude or could be too friendly and sympathetic to the customer, giving away too much time or information. Putting distance between the client and the technician gives the dealership management greater control over the relationship and the process.[40]

Economic and Work Environment

The work in a typical dealership is busy and stressful. The hours are long, with some managers and owners putting in up to eighty hours a week. With the long hours and intense pressure, tempers can fray easily and quickly—it only takes a relatively minor problem or frustration for conversations to change from good-natured joking to testy sarcasm.

The source of tension in a dealership stems from two major cultural attitudes. The first is the intense focus on profits that creates an atmosphere in which, as one manager said, "The almighty dollar rules." This is not an unusual attitude in the business world, but automobile dealers have a somewhat unusual accounting requirement—many dealerships work on a thirty-day cycle, meaning that they close out the books twelve times a year. The result is that people are judged on what they did in the past thirty days only, and as a consequence there is often little incentive for long-term planning. Time is money, and there is an ongoing and constant calculation of financial payoff for any new idea. Owners and managers weigh the payoff against the investment—obviously a wise thing to do in any business—but the focus is strictly on the short term. Even if an innovation has the potential for a large payoff, if that payoff is delayed for several months or a year, it could easily be rejected. The situation, further aggravated by the increased competition and cost-cutting of the past decade, has made some managers feel that their jobs have been reduced to "fire fighting" rather than management, and that any creativity and flexibility they once had is rapidly disappearing. Sales are the bottom line in a dealership, and as one person wryly noted there are endless awards for quantity of sales but none for the quality of management.

In addition to the relentless focus on short-term profit is the vague but constant fear of being reprimanded or penalized. Employees worry about managers, managers worry about owners, and owners worry about the head office. Employees at all levels worry that if they express their opinions openly and honestly, especially if that opinion reveals criticism of current policy, the manufacturer or the dealership owner will retaliate. Because this distrust permeates the workplace, employees hesitate to suggest new ideas or volunteer any information.

The organizational structure is strictly top-down. The head office sends dictates to the dealerships, and in the dealership information is expected to flow from the owner to the managers to the employees. An example of a suggestion moving from an employee at the bottom up through the chain of command is rare. Innovation is not encouraged in this culture. And many managers believe that employees are only motivated by money.

Dealership employees often claim that their work is unrewarding (other than financially), unfulfilling, and discouraging of creativity or innovation. Yet in spite of the difficulties and limitations, when asked what they like about the work, most employees first describe their love of cars and then explain how they enjoy the nonroutine aspect of their jobs. As they say, "no day is typical." They like the challenge of their work, and they are proud of what they do.

SERVICE ADVISORS

The atmosphere of the service department is usually very busy, but things get particularly hectic in the morning when customers are dropping off their cars, and again in the evening when they are picking them up. Sometimes it can be outright chaotic. The service department is set up to be very busy when everything is going well, and consequently there is little margin for error. When minor things go wrong, they can have major repercussions. And minor and occasionally major emergencies do happen—regularly, but unpredictably. Several technicians can be out sick with the flu. The power can go off. There can be a series of unreasonable customers. Computers crash. Phones go down. Service advisors have to take it all in stride. There are periodic five-minute lulls when the phones stop ringing and no customers come in. During these periods service advisors will try to catch up on their work, doing follow-up, checking prices, and completing paperwork, all interspersed with good-natured joking and chatting. The telephone is in constant use. Because of this hectic pace, service advisors require focus, concentration, and a good memory. They juggle dozens of tasks generated by a constant stream of people demanding their attention—either customers, technicians, or other dealership employees walking in or phoning them to ask questions.

Service advisors are usually paid a salary plus a commission. The commission is a percentage of the sales (parts and labor), and in some dealerships that can make up a good proportion of their take-home pay. For example, in the Boston area, the annual income for service advisors is in the mid-$50,000 range.[41] "Not bad for someone with a high-school education," as one manager observed. Clearly though, having a significant percentage of their salary come from commission puts them in an ambiguous and contradictory position. On one hand they are supposed to be "advisors" to the customer, but on the other, they have a financial incentive to sell more parts and services than may be absolutely necessary.

PARTS EMPLOYEES

The atmosphere in the parts department is always busy and fast-paced, yet there is still an underlying sense of order and calm. Though the work is often more predictable than at the service counter, it is certainly never routine—an aspect that the staff enjoys. The parts employees are in constant motion, either looking up parts on the computer, locating them on the shelves, or bringing them back to the counter. No one sits down and there are few breaks. During the rare times when they are not on the phone, talking to a customer, or picking up parts, they do paperwork and assemble orders that will be picked up later in the day.[42]

The parts employees earn an hourly wage as well as a commission. Though they do not have much control over the quantity of parts used by the technicians, and therefore their commission, they can influence the sales of their retail and wholesale customers.

Technicians are paid in a variety of ways—by salary, by the hour, or by the job—depending on the shop policy and the technician's preference and experience. If A-level technicians are paid hourly, the rate would depend on whether they are working on warranty or nonwarranty work. When working on warranty work they are often paid on the flat-rate system based on Chilton's auto repair manuals that assigns the amount of time a competent technician should require to complete a standard repair task. This means that if Chilton estimates a repair job to take two hours, and the technician completes it in less time, the technician is still paid for the two hours of work. Of course, if it takes more than the estimated two hours, he will still only be paid for the two hours. This means that an experienced technician has the potential to get paid for sixty to seventy hours worth of work in a fifty-hour week. Nonwarranty work is often paid by the clock, meaning that the customer pays the dealership for as many hours as it takes to make the repair.[43]

SALESPEOPLE

In the service department, customers and staff may have very different views of what constitutes a problem, but in the sales department, salespeople and customers have very different perspectives on prices of vehicles. Customers generally see the purchase of a vehicle as an enormous, even momentous decision and investment, probably only next in scale to buying a home. Sales reps, on the other hand, become hardened or desensitized to just how costly cars are. One sales manager acknowledged that they sometimes forget just how expensive a car is for the average household. Other sales reps are outright unsympathetic. When asked about the high cost of buying a vehicle, one sales rep said "So what—if they don't like it, they should buy a bike." As insensitive as this sounds, salespeople do quickly become accustomed to the large numbers because from their perspective a $25,000 vehicle is really only worth a few hundred dollars since that is all they will make as commission on the sale. In spite of the high prices of the vehicles, the sales department does not make a large profit on each one. Sales reps earn a percentage—between 20 and 30 percent—of the difference between the sale price and the dealer invoice (Genat 1999: 94). For example, if a vehicle's invoice price is $25,000 and it is sold at 3 percent over invoice (that is, $25,750), the dealership earns $750. Of that, the salesperson would receive $187 plus a base of approximately $50 for a total of $262—not a large sum for a sale that might have taken many hours of work. If the customer pays the dealer invoice price (a case that can occasionally occur), the salesperson receives nothing, except perhaps a sales bonus offered by the manufacturer. The system certainly explains salespeoples' efforts to push the prices as high as possible, their attempts to encourage the sales of higher-priced vehicles, and the intense pressure they are under to maximize sales volume.[44] Because salespeople receive relatively little per transaction, they need to compensate with volume.[45]

Many of the manufacturers are now toying with the idea of improving the payment system, and many sales managers and reps are open to the idea of a nonnegotiable single price—they say that it would be simpler and less stressful for all concerned.[46] What worries them, however, is who sets the price and where the price is set. It is not that they are against the idea, but they are very anxious to ensure that dealers and salespeople can still make a fair profit and reasonable income.

The salary structure is an obstacle for some of the dealership employees, but especially for the salespeople. For other groups, there are other problems, but as we can see, all the workgroups face at least some, if not all, of the six obstacles to learning and communication.

CHAPTER FIVE

Synthesis and Evaluation

Describing the past and present work practices in automobile dealerships is easily recognizable as the data-collection step of the design process. The collected data allow us to confidently declare that GFC and its dealerships, as they are now, are definitely not learning communities, and it is obvious that all would benefit if more communication and learning could occur. We also can see that the problem lies not with the personal failings or attitudes of individual employees, but with the work environment itself. Holding up GFC or the auto industry as failures in terms of their attempts to become learning organizations is not the purpose of describing the messy problems and complicated relationships that exist in the workplace and the obstacles that are faced. Instead, GFC's experience is helpful because it illustrates how the workplace is much more subtle and nuanced than first imagined, and it begins to hint at some of the steps that might be necessary to create the conditions for functional learning and effective communication to occur.

The second step in the design process is problem identification and analysis, and we have looked at the work practices of GFC dealerships in some detail and analyzed the challenges they face in terms of the physical environment, the medium, the content, the individual, the cultural and social environment, and the economic and work environment. The next stages are synthesis and evaluation. It is useful to repeat the point made earlier that the model of Data Collection → Analysis → Synthesis → Evaluation is accurate in that these functions do take place and more or less in that order, but this is also overly simplistic and linear. In reality the design process does not always fit into these neat and logical activities, and in practice it can be nonsequential, iterative, and much more untidy.

The next two stages, synthesis or proposal and evaluation, essentially involve pulling together the disparate threads of the problem and creating a possible response or set of responses, followed by an evaluation, which weights the proposed solution in terms of its likelihood to succeed within the given context.

Obstacles to Learning and Communication

GFC's head office in Detroit was keen to create and support communities of practice, to encourage communication between the head office and the dealerships as well as between and within dealerships, and to become more of a learning organization. It seemed like a worthwhile goal that would benefit all, but the dealers were perceived as being unenthusiastic about the prospect and not good team players. GFC wanted to know what the problem was with the dealers and how they could get them to buy into the vision.

The literature gives much to consider when deciding whether a firm is a learning organization or not. There are many possible attributes of a learning organization, but in applying just five of the main ones—clarity of mission and purpose, shared leadership and involvement, experimentation, transfer of knowledge, and teamwork and cooperation (Goh 2001)—to the dealerships' work environment and practice, we can see that GFC dealerships would score fairly low and would not be considered learning organizations.

The literature on IT points out that the adoption of technology in the workplace is not a question of all or nothing. Technology can be rejected or it can adopted on a continuum from minimal to whole-hearted, and the level of adoption is not necessarily a reflection on the firm or the individual. Non-adoption or reluctance to adopt information technology is less likely to be due to employees who are backward, uncreative, and rigid, and more likely to be linked to their status, role, and environment. And finally, the communication and IT literature tell us that technology can be enormously helpful in creating the means for work colleagues to communicate and collaborate, but those benefits are by no means automatic and cannot be taken for granted.

The literature on both organizational learning and IT adoption (such as Allard 1998; Dilworth 1996; Redding 1997; Reger and von Wichert-Nick 1997; Senge 1990, 1994; Wenger 1998; and Wenger, McDermott, and Snyder 2002) may be useful for identifying firms and organizations with certain characteristics, but as others have complained before, it is not very helpful for suggesting ways of getting there.

Given what we know about the state of work, environment, and culture at GFC dealerships, and the major obstacles to sharing of knowledge, it might be logical, reasonable, and easy to conclude that GFC's goal is simply unattainable. But despair would not be completely warranted. Glimmers of hope remain in this clearly dysfunctional work environment. Communication and learning—both formal and informal—do take place in all departments. The parts department, for example, has even managed to be relatively successful at creating an environment that enables or promotes the sharing of information. It possesses a number of important characteristics such as the atmosphere, pay structure, use of IT, attitude toward learning, and makeup of its community that contribute to an environment that is amenable to sharing information and makes employees better candidates for learning and sharing of knowledge between the dealership and Detroit, and between dealerships. If it can happen there, perhaps it can happen in the other departments.

The real question is not "What is wrong with the dealers who are preventing GFC from becoming a learning organization?" but "What steps can be taken to improve communication and sharing of knowledge within the organization?" One question incorrectly places blame on the employees, and the other focuses on taking positive steps to reaching a goal.

At this stage, it is worth quickly summarizing the key work conditions and challenges across the dealership departments. Again, the purpose of identifying the barriers or obstacles is not to emphasize the negative, but to accurately shape the problem statement in order to point toward solutions.

PHYSICAL ENVIRONMENT

The flow of information between colleagues may be inhibited simply because of physical distance, isolation, or a noisy environment that prevents communication.

The physical environment of automobile dealerships is generally not an obstacle to the flow of information between colleagues in the dealership except in the case of the technicians, whose service bays are usually spread apart and whose environment can be noisy. They overcome their inability to converse by "forgetting" to order their spare parts ahead of time and using the time waiting at the parts counter to chat with each other. Other dealership employees (service advisors, parts employees, and salespeople) work in favorable conditions for conversing—a relatively quiet workplace and in fairly close proximity.

MEDIUM

Though there is both a system for and an extensive flow of information from GFC Detroit to the dealerships, the reverse flow from the dealerships to Detroit is much more limited. Technicians can communicate with the engineers at the head office through their online system and a phone-in helpline, though they may sometimes be reluctant to use them because of issues of time, pay structure, or negative past experience. The managers in the parts department do not have an online system in the workplace, but they have organized themselves and developed an administrative system that allows for their concerns to be communicated directly with the head office in Detroit without making the individual dealership a target for punishment. Because the concerns, suggestions, and complaints are shared by a larger group, individuals cannot be singled out as troublemakers, and this allows them to anonymously and therefore "safely" express their concerns to the head office. With this arrangement, the Detroit office gets the information it needs, and the parts departments are safe from retaliation. Departmental service and sales managers can also communicate with the manufacturer's regional field staff, but their concerns may or may not always be reliably transmitted farther up the hierarchy. The rest of the dealership employees have little or no way of communicating their concerns or sharing their knowledge with the manufacturer in Detroit. It is true that in theory they have the opportunity to communicate with the hosts of the Distance Education System programs, but this is an unsatisfactory option given the few times they take the class per year and the difficulty of connecting to the host when they are in the class.

Communication between dealerships is very limited. There are very few events organized by the manufacturer for employees from local dealerships to meet, and as training has migrated from centralized or regional training facilities to the individual's worksite, there is even less opportunity. Some employees and ex-employees have created Websites, independent of and unsanctioned by GFC, that can be used to exchange information among dealership employees. These Websites are sometimes highly critical of the manufacturer's policies and labor practices, and tend to have more technicians and parts employees participating than service advisors and salespeople. It is unclear, however, how effective this is as a means of communicating with the manufacturer or how widely it is read by dealership employees or those at the head office, outside of the legal department, which periodically sues them for inflammatory or libelous statements.

At the level of the dealership, using information technology (IT) in the workplace to promote communication with the head office in Detroit poses an additional problem because of the dealers' past experience. The very medium that GFC wants to use to cultivate a learning community is a sore point for many dealers, and their experience with IT over the past years has left a bitter taste in their mouths. Dealers associate IT with outrageous expense, and it symbolizes their helplessness and lack of control over their own business. As long as dealers are forced to pay for equipment and software at what they perceive to be inflated prices, then receive inadequate support and have to use outdated and user-unfriendly software, it is difficult to imagine dealers readily and enthusiastically embracing new technologies or extending the use of existing ones.

Though there is no overt hostility toward information technology, dealing with it is apparently not the dealership employees' favorite pastime. Not only is there a confusing mix of hardware and software, but it tends to be awkward and difficult to use. Employees often state that they are uncomfortable and hesitant using the system because they are not sure of its capabilities. Accessibility to the Internet is limited in most dealerships; most employees do not have e-mail and rarely have easy access to the Internet, though connectivity and accessibility are certainly rapidly increasing, and most of their databases and information will likely soon all be Internet- or Web-based.

Each workgroup has a different relationship with IT. The parts employees use a variety of information technologies in their work and regularly consult the in-house system for current inventory as well as informational CDs for retrieving part numbers and illustrations, locating parts in the inventories of local dealerships, and ordering new stock from GFC in Detroit. For the technicians, IT plays an important role in their work: computers are an integral part of today's vehicles, and technicians also use a series of diagnostic tools and computers to repair and maintain those vehicles. In the service department, service advisors are the heaviest users of the in-house computer system for keeping track of appointments and work orders. Though the system is awkward, they do learn to use it, and they also make extensive use of the telephone for contacting customers as well as their colleagues in other departments within the dealership. The sales department uses IT less than any other workgroup in the dealership, though there may be a computer on the floor that is used for calculating lease payments or special ordering a vehicle, and the sales manager would certainly have a computer on his desk.

CONTENT

The Distance Education System (DES) programming for technicians benefits them in very practical ways by helping them correctly diagnose and quickly repair a vehicle. Not surprisingly, technicians have a fairly positive attitude toward the formal learning. Because their work is so often nonroutine and challenging, they also rely on informal learning from their fellow technicians. In addition, of all the dealership employees, technicians are the most likely candidates to participate in hands-on training courses organized by the manufacturer at regional training centers, which they see as a positive opportunity to upgrade their skills and increase their salaries.

The parts department also has a fairly positive attitude toward both formal and informal learning. The DES programs generally focus on the practical aspects of running a parts department and managing the complicated inventory system, which in turn helps employees work more quickly and effectively. Learning informally from their colleagues is crucial and is the primary means for employees to learn how to do their jobs.

Though the service advisors may not have any active antipathy toward formal DES training, unlike the technicians or parts employees, the immediate benefit or payoff gained from the training is not as apparent to them. Because much of the programming focuses on how to relate to and serve customers better, it may indirectly help them by reducing the tension in their transactions with the customer, and in the long term a happier customer is more likely to return, but in the short term, the advisors are unlikely to see a noticeable increase in their income or improvement in their daily work because of the DES training programs.

The salespeople are generally the most hostile to the formal DES training programs. They reject the formal training for a number of reasons. First, embedded in the sales culture is the belief that the best salespeople already possess the raw charismatic quality and drive that is necessary for their success and is something that cannot be taught. Second, much of the training programs' current content focuses on trying to change salespeople's deeply held attitudes, their culture, and their relationship with customers. The message they are given is that their work should become more service-oriented, and that the tactics and expertise they have gained over the years may now be irrelevant. Not only does this threaten their self-image, but they fear that a service orientation may bring a single-price model—something that potentially could mean a significant loss of income for them. The result, not surprisingly, is that salespeople are often much less enthused about learning and training. Because they feel threatened by the material in the training programs, they tend to reject both the message and the messenger.

The content or information sent through a medium may be negative or positive, but in order for shared learning to take place one also needs to know what type of information is required and who needs it. In the case of technicians, it is fairly clear: the GFC engineering department in Detroit wants to hear from the technicians so that it can give them advance warning of technical problems and suggest ways to repair them—information that can then be passed on to other technicians around the country. Consequently, it has created the most structured opportunities for technicians to communicate with the head office. Despite the opportunities though, technicians often do not avail themselves of them because the reward for sharing information with the head office does not always compensate for the effort it takes—the system can be slow and awkward, and their past experience of communicating with the manufacturer has not always been positive. For the rest of the dealership employees, it is not at all clear what type of information the Detroit head office would like to receive from them or who there would be interested in their knowledge. In the case of salespeople, the underlying message from Detroit is that there is almost no knowledge that they want from them.

INDIVIDUAL

Attitudes toward informal and formal learning and communication vary with the type of work, but they can also vary with an individual's personality and experience. For example, even though salespeople in general are the most resistant to formal learning, there can be an individual within the group who displays great enthusiasm for both formal and informal training. And the technicians with greater experience tend to be the ones who are most reluctant to participate in the formal communication and feedback programs promoted by the manufacturer, mostly because they see it as a waste of their time and not particularly advantageous financially.

CULTURAL AND SOCIAL ENVIRONMENT

If there is an adversarial attitude between groups, or if a group believes that sharing information will harm them in some way, there is likely to be no sharing of information. GFC and its dealerships illustrate how embedded this division can be. First, there is the fundamental structural problem resulting from the fact that dealers are independent businesspeople, not employees of the manufacturer. There are many advantages to this arrangement, especially for the manufacturer, including the ability to hand off responsibility for sales and service to the dealers. It allows the managers in Detroit to retain some control and influence, but they do not have to deal with the daily problems of servicing their vehicles. On the downside, the manufacturer makes it very clear that there is a sharp dividing line between Detroit and the dealers, with the dealership employees receiving fewer benefits and regard than those based in the head office, making them, in the eyes of dealership employees, second-class citizens. To sour the relationship further, dealers often perceive GFC as manipulating the boundary between them to its advantage. The dealers perceive the manufacturer as crossing the line and interfering with their private business, and then stepping back or withdrawing to safety, claiming separation, when it suits them.

This atmosphere of distrust between the factory and its stores discourages learning and communication. Both the head office and the dealerships understand that they would all benefit from better communication and sharing of knowledge, but accomplishing this would mean unraveling years of suspicion and distrust on both sides. An unease permeates the work environment. Dealers fear retaliation from Detroit if they act or say something deemed unacceptable by the head office. The same atmosphere is duplicated within the dealership itself, with employees always wary of saying or doing something wrong, or expressing an opinion that might offend their employers. It takes little imagination to see that in any situation in which employees feel that their job security depends on keeping quiet, the chance that staff will enthusiastically volunteer information or share knowledge is very low indeed.

The communication within this organization is typical of many large corporations. The "natural" flow of information is top-down, and the opinions of subordinates are rarely solicited or listened to. GFC issues decrees to the dealers, and dealers deliver decrees to their employees. Neither the head office nor most dealers encourage two-way communication, even though they may intellectually understand that this would be beneficial. There are some exceptions, however. As described earlier, the parts managers have organized themselves into a regional professional group and have created ways of presenting their concerns to the head office that do not jeopardize or identify the individual or the dealership. And some dealership employees do talk among themselves online, again safely with anonymity, but not directly to their employers or to the Detroit managers. Of all the employees in a dealership, service advisors are the communicators and "sharers" of knowledge. They constantly monitor and help each other throughout the day, and most of their training is done by working with more experienced advisors and gradually participating in the daily work routine. Despite being the communicators within the dealership, they have almost no contact with the manufacturer, and the head office has given little indication that it is interested in the knowledge that the service advisors have to share.

In the auto industry's culture, learning is also understood in rather traditional and hierarchical terms—as a process of transmission and internalization. The teacher is seen as the fount of knowledge, and the knowledge flows in a one-way direction toward the student, who receives and absorbs the information. Learning is generally not seen as a social process or considered in the context of work or relationships. As it is, the current training system focuses more on instruction than learning.

Each of the workgroups within a dealership is part of a broader professional or work-based community, but with significant differences between them (Figure 5.1).

The technicians' work community is usually made up of their immediate colleagues and, to a lesser extent, the parts employees and service advisors. They have very little contact with the rest of the dealership staff and even less with the technicians in nearby dealerships, except for the individuals who have maintained friendships and social relations with technicians with whom they have worked in the past.

The parts employees' work community is primarily dealership-based, but they also actively maintain a cordial professional relationship with parts departments in other local dealerships, and have developed an informal cooperative system in which they can buy parts from each other when they need to procure a part immediately. Many of the parts department managers who belong to their professional group also connect at a regional level.

The service advisors have the widest range of community within the dealership; they are the only employees who communicate with colleagues outside their department on a regular basis. Though they are usually at the service counter, it is not unusual for them to walk back into the shop or the parts department, or over to sales if they need a quick answer to a question.

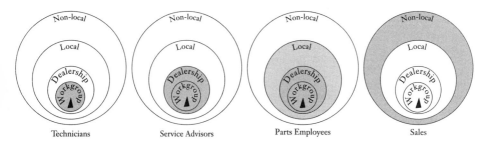

Figure 5.1. Dealership employees' professional communities

As a result, service advisors know almost every employee in the dealership. Their sense of community is limited to their own dealership, however, and they have little contact with the service departments of other local dealerships.

The sales employees have the most limited work community of all the dealership employees. Because they are in competition with each other for customers, there is a reluctance to share knowledge. Though they are likely to maintain a civil or cordial relationship with their colleagues, they are often not close either professionally or socially. In addition, they have limited contact with the other departments in the dealership, and tend to see themselves as an island of white-collar professionals in a blue-collar dealership. Salespeople are also in fierce competition with other local dealerships, so almost no communication or sharing of knowledge occurs between them. The only people with whom they do not compete, and have a great deal in common, are salespeople in dealerships located in other regions.

An important part of the cultural environment and social atmosphere in the dealership is created by the employees' relationship with the customer, and each of the dealership workgroups has quite different relationships and roles. The technicians have the least direct contact with customers—an intentional policy on the part of dealership managers, who fear that contact between technicians and customers will be bad for business either because the technicians' perceived lack of social skills will offend customers, or their gregarious and generous nature will make them empathize with the customer and give away too much information or work for free.

The parts employees have fairly limited contact, but what contact they do have is straightforward. A customer comes in, requests a spare part, and buys the part for a known price. There is no haggling, and the only discussion between them would involve verifying that the customer is indeed getting the correct part or assembly that he or she needs.

In contrast, the service advisors have almost constant contact with customers and are trained to be social and friendly with the customer while always keeping the dealership's interests uppermost in their minds. The relationship is conflicted because they are supposed to be "advisors" to the customer, yet they could easily benefit financially by misadvising customers or overstating the repair needs of their vehicles and selling more parts and services than may be absolutely necessary.

For the salespeople, customers are both a coveted resource and their greatest irritation. Salesmen may act in a warm and friendly manner toward customers in order to encourage them to buy a vehicle, but of course they do not have the best interests of the customer at heart. To succeed at their job, salespeople must get the customers to pay as much as they possibly can. They dislike customers who come to the dealership expecting the worst from the salespeople, and also despise those customers who come in prepared and able to negotiate down to the lowest possible price. Their dream customers, and they are few and far between these days, are those who naively but cheerfully pay as close as possible to the manufacturer's recommended price.

ECONOMIC AND WORK ENVIRONMENT

One of the most striking characteristics of dealership life, especially for the service-oriented workgroups, is the hectic pace that is maintained all day long. Because employees are so busy with their daily tasks, many barely have time for lunch or breaks, never mind time for leisurely reflection, thoughtful contemplation, or sharing of best practices. And understandably, once they leave the dealership after a long and tiring day, most are not inclined to use their leisure or family time for work purposes.

The automobile industry sees competition as one of the strongest and most important attributes that drives the business. Without it, the assumption is that dealers and manufacturers would not be as motivated to produce and sell vehicles. Unfortunately the same competition that drives the industry to produce and sell more product can also undermine the whole foundation of collaboration and sharing of information. If firms or individuals are in direct competition with each other, there is almost no reason to share knowledge. The sales department engages in fierce competition with local dealerships, as do its own salespeople with each other, which means that there is every reason to conceal information, best practices, or lessons learned from colleagues and local competitors. There is an exception to this rule, however. Because customers tend to only buy vehicles locally, dealers would likely have much less objection to an employee offering a suggestion that benefited another dealership on the other side of the country as long as they felt that they might receive the same benefit in return one day.

With the other workgroups, competition with colleagues in nearby dealerships varies. Technicians are the most insulated from any competition. How well they do their job does not have much of an impact on technicians in another dealership, except perhaps indirectly. For the service advisors,

TABLE 5.1

Summary of characteristics, opportunities, and obstacles to the flow of information and sharing of knowledge

PHYSICAL ENVIRONMENT

	Technicians	Service Advisors	Parts Employees	Salespeople
Exchange of information between colleagues	Negative; not conducive to flow of information between technicians; distance between bays; noisy	Positive; work in close proximity; quiet	Positive; work in close proximity; relatively quiet	Positive; work in relatively close proximity; quiet

MEDIUM

	Technicians	Service Advisors	Parts Employees	Salespeople
Between Detroit and dealerships	Somewhat positive; have most electronic systems in place for reporting technical problems and solutions	Negative; no communication system in place	Somewhat positive; have administrative systems in place	Negative; no communication system in place
Between dealerships, locally and regionally	Very limited; occasional use of Websites	None	Some through cooperative parts purchasing system, and parts managers group	Very limited; occasional participation in manufacturer-sponsored events
Existing IT systems	Neutral; extensively used, but can be awkward	Negative; generally poor past experience; poor quality support; expensive; awkward or slow systems		
Daily IT use	High to very high	Moderate	High	Very limited
E-mail or Internet access	Negative; often not readily available, but improving			
Overall attitude to IT	Expensive, difficult to use, confusing mix of software and hardware; increasing access to Internet; no overt hostility to technology			

CONTENT

	Technicians	Service Advisors	Parts Employees	Salespeople
Content of Distance Education System (DES) training programs	Positive; helps them to do repairs more quickly; of direct benefit	Mixed; focuses on improving their relationship with the customer; does not benefit them directly	Positive; information is general, practical, and useful; helps them do their work faster and easier	Negative; information is threatening; belief that sales cannot be taught
	Difficult planning and scheduling because of conflict with daily schedule; amount of training required is not extensive			
Dealerships to Detroit	Positive; fairly clear what type of information head office is looking for	Negative; not clear what type of information head office wants from these employees, who needs it, or who would use it		

INDIVIDUAL

	Technicians	Service Advisors	Parts Employees	Salespeople
	Mixed; every individual will have different attitudes about learning and sharing knowledge, and have a different experience of having done so in the past; also, their willingness to give or receive information will depend on their position within the dealership			

CULTURAL AND SOCIAL ENVIRONMENT

	Technicians	Service Advisors	Parts Employees	Salespeople
View of manufacturer-dealership relationship	Often negative; dealers are not considered equal partners; dealers perceive GFC as unsympathetic to their situation; suspect that head office changes the rules for its own benefit and misuse of power			
Flow of information between Detroit and dealerships	Negative; top-down seen as natural flow; opinions that challenge the status quo are discouraged			

TABLE 5.1 (*continued*)

CULTURAL AND SOCIAL ENVIRONMENT

	Technicians	Service Advisors	Parts Employees	Salespeople
Flow of communication between colleagues	Moderate between technicians, limited by environment; high potential between technicians and Detroit engineers	Very high level between advisors; fairly high between other employees in dealership	Fairly high between parts employees; contact with local and regional colleagues	Little between salespeople
Attitude to formal learning	Top-down is seen as the "natural" flow of information			
	Learning is considered in traditional terms			
	Relatively positive	Relatively positive	Relatively positive	Negative
Informal learning between colleagues	Fairly high, but limited by physical environment	Very high	High	Very low
Professional community	Workgroup-based	Workgroup and dealership-based	Workgroup and locally based	Little sense of community; potential only with nonlocal colleagues
Contact with customers	Very limited or none	Constant interaction	Varies with the type of dealership, but is often fairly low	High
Relationship with customers	None	Ambiguous; divided loyalties	Straightforward transactions	Ambiguous; desires them, but finds them frustrating

ECONOMIC AND WORK ENVIRONMENT

	Technicians	Service Advisors	Parts Employees	Salespeople
Work atmosphere	Busy, but usually relatively calm	Hectic and stressful	Busy, but usually calm with some stressful periods	Calm, but personally stressful
	Negative; overwhelming emphasis on short-term profit; risk-averse			
	Vague but constant fear about saying or doing the wrong thing, and of retribution by superiors; rigidly top-down			
Pace of work	Negative; usually hectic; long hours			Mixed; variable pace; long hours
Competition between colleagues	Low or no competition	Low or no competition	Low or no competition	High competition; compete with each other for customers
Competition between local dealerships	Minimal or no competition	Mixed; some competition, but not a worry	Positive; low or no competition; cooperation is common	Negative; high competition
Salary and financial incentives	Mixed; often paid flat rate for warranty work and hourly wage for non-warranty, but can vary with individual and dealership	Mixed; most are paid by salary plus percentage of sales	Mixed; most are paid salary plus percentage of sales; limited control over sales	Negative; usually are paid by commission only
	Overwhelming focus on profit at the end of the month; conservative; risk-averse			

there is some competition between dealerships because there is a finite number of customers available, but for the most part, they do not seem to worry about it a great deal. For the parts employees, the situation is somewhat unusual because they have an almost cooperative relationship with their fellow parts departments in other local dealerships. Their dealerships may compete for customers, but the parts departments think nothing of asking their competitors for help in providing an out-of-stock spare part, and they would readily return the favor if asked.

The salary system also conspires against the flow of information, but the salary and financial incentives vary considerably among the workgroups. Many employees receive a percentage of the sales made in their departments, and for some their entire salary is based on commission. Parts employees are often paid on an hourly basis, sometimes with a percentage of the sales to the public, but the commission income usually makes up a less significant proportion of their salary. The technicians, valued by both the dealers and the manufacturer, are quite well paid—either by the hour or a flat rate, depending on the policy of the shop, their level of expertise, and the type of work they are doing. Those who are paid a flat rate are the least likely to take the time to share knowledge because the faster they finish the job the more they will earn, but those who receive a salary or hourly wage may be more open to taking the time to communicate with others. The problem, however, is that hourly employees often are the least experienced employees, and hence the quality of information they share may be less valuable. Service advisors are usually paid by the hour plus a percentage of the shop's revenue, and for some, this commission can make up a substantial part of their income. Most salespeople work entirely on commission, which means that the more they sell and the higher the price they can get for the vehicle, the more they will earn.

Because so many employees' salaries are based at least in part on commission, any time spent online, learning, or communicating with others is time for which they are earning either a reduced or no salary. The more time they spend communicating with Detroit or supporting and cultivating a community of practice, the less money they will make—hardly an effective way to encourage employees to share their knowledge, especially in a group so motivated by financial incentives.

The complete and utter focus on the bottom line and on generating a profit for the dealership at the end of each month also works against learning, communicating, and sharing of knowledge. Any activity that does not contribute directly toward the monthly statement is actively discouraged. Even though it is quite clear to all that sharing dealership experience with the Detroit office will pay off in the long run with better vehicles and better policies, it is the short term that preoccupies dealers because that is how they are judged by GFC. Because of this system, dealers who tend to view themselves as exceptional risk-takers are loath to experiment with anything that might jeopardize their monthly report. The short-term focus on profits manages to turn them into risk-averse and conservative managers.

Designing Solutions

The literature on learning and information technology in the workplace comes from a variety of disciplines ranging from management to anthropology to sociology, and, similar to Argyris and Schön's observation about organizational learning (1978, 1996), their positions usually fall into one of two categories. The first is to exhort firms to become learning organizations, and it is hard to disagree with the notion that communicating and learning from each other within the workplace would be beneficial for both the organization and the individual. The other category of the literature is much more judgmental, declaring a firm to be a learning organization or not depending on a set of attributes. From this perspective, organizations either have it or do not, much like salesmen who just have the "right stuff." There is nothing particularly wrong with either of these positions, but they are rather unhelpful in a practical sense for those firms that do want to increase learning and communication because they give little in the way of guidance on how to achieve the goal.

For many fields and disciplines, the purpose of looking so closely at a work environment and work practices is simply to expand the current understanding of the workplace and the people in it. That, on its own, is a valuable contribution, but those coming from a design background tend to look at the rich detail gained from ethnological studies through a somewhat different set of lenses. A deep and subtle understanding of the workplace is not an end in itself, but is rather the raw material to be used for creating a solution or set of solutions. For design-oriented managers, the purpose of such a study is not to judge, but to find ways of creating an environment that will support learning and communication within an organization such as GFC and between it and its dealerships.

For example, if we view a firm's problems with learning and communication not as a litmus test but as a process or a continuum, it becomes possible to imagine a way forward and to suggest steps that can be taken to improve the situation. Applying the design process in the case of GFC would generate ideas or strategies that this manufacturer and its dealerships (or any firm in a similar situation) could take to move toward becoming more of a learning organization and communicating more effectively with each other.

The obstacles faced by GFC and its dealerships in terms of sharing knowledge are many. Some of the work groups simply do not have the means of communicating, either with the Detroit office or each other. Some of the content in the DES classes for some workgroups is very pertinent, while for others the message undermines their status and control. All dealership employees work in an environment that focuses on profit, and communication simply does not fit easily into the economic equation. Work days are generally hectic and long, competition is intense, and the culture is one that has never been conducive to exchanging information and learning.

Given the business context, history, and obstacles faced by GFC, there are two main approaches that it could take. One approach, that should not be discounted, is to accept the existing system more or less as it is, or to tinker with it in some minor way; that is, to improve learning and communicating in the workplace without making any fundamental changes. Though the payoff may not be as great, in some cases this may be the only option that a firm has, or believes it has.

The second approach is to make changes at a much more fundamental level—changes that alter the very structure and model of how GFC relates to the dealerships and how they both relate to the customer. At this level, it would be a matter of figuring out how to cut the Gordian knot of competitiveness and adversarial relationships and create an environment that is substantially different from the dysfunctional one that exists today. Information technology can play a significant role in achieving some of these changes and increasing learning and communication, but IT is not the only solution. Some of the more effective actions that GFC could take would involve changing basic policy and cultural attitudes.

The benefits of any change will not always be equally shared. Some may accrue to certain groups within the dealership, while others may be spread more widely. And change at any level, no matter how beneficial, will also come at some financial or social cost, or both. On the basis of the obstacles faced by this firm and its dealerships, and assuming that the existing business model remains the same, there are a number of steps that GFC could take to improve the flow of information.

PHYSICAL ENVIRONMENT

The physical quality of a place does matter. Dealers could contribute to increased enthusiasm for formal learning by simply *improving the DES training rooms.* These rooms should not give the impression that training and learning are unimportant and vaguely shameful activities that take place in a remote leftover corner of the dealership. Instead, the rooms should be professional looking, pleasant, light, and comfortable. Dealers could even place the training room in a prominent and visible place in the dealership in order to demonstrate to customers (and employees) that ongoing learning is taken seriously. The Detroit office can certainly encourage dealers to make these changes by providing planning and building guidelines when dealers are renovating, as well as with financial incentives such as equipment, rebates, or cash.

MEDIUM

Provide Internet access at work. Because most dealership employees have no means of communicating with Detroit or their colleagues in other dealerships, the first step would be to provide Internet access and e-mail accounts in the workplace for every employee. Though employees are normally very busy all day with their work tasks and activities, a computer with Internet access could be installed in the lunchroom or common area where employees could pick up e-mail, use the Web, or participate in online discussion during breaks or off-hours. This action would permit an easier flow of information between the head office and dealership employees, or between dealerships, but on the downside it might also threaten those in the dealership management hierarchy who would be bypassed in the process. In addition, there is always the concern of managers that employees will waste time on personal e-mail or just surfing the Internet.

   Permit flexibility in equipment and software procurement. Computer and communication technology has long been a sore point with GFC dealerships.

Forcing the dealerships to purchase equipment at high prices from only a re-stricted number of suppliers who offer poor technical support has under-standably made dealership managers and owners nervous and hesitant, if not outright hostile. The policy of limiting suppliers made sense in the early 1990s, when the World Wide Web barely existed, but since then the tech-nology has vastly improved and the cost of equipment and software has plummeted. GFC needs to abandon this policy and allow dealers to take ad-vantage of the lower-priced hardware and software now available. It is per-fectly reasonable for GFC to set certain equipment standards in terms of memory, functionality, hard drive size, broadband capacity, and so on, in or-der to ensure compatibility and interoperability, but many other choices such as the manufacturer, platform, and supplier could be left to the dealer.

It would also be tremendously useful if the different computer systems in the dealership with their different operating systems could be consolidated into a single-access, multipurpose networked system.

And finally, the Detroit managers could also make a conciliatory gesture to help compensate for the years of insisting that dealers purchase over-priced equipment by sharing the cost of any new replacement hardware or software.

Develop user-friendly software. The software that dealership employees cur-rently use on a daily basis is generally awkward and slow. With the move to commercially available computers, new applications should be designed us-ing readily available software. These applications should also be designed and tested with the active involvement of the employees who will use them. GFC could choose several dealerships, pay them to participate in the exper-iment, test the software, and resolve any problems before widespread imple-mentation. Not only would this result in a much better product, but it would help reassure the dealers that their opinions matter to the head office, and that the Detroit managers care about the quality of the software that the dealerships have to use.

Improve the Technical Helpline. Though the response time of the "Help-line," the system technicians use to call in with a specific question or prob-lem, has improved every year, it still needs to continue to improve. First and foremost the system needs to be faster and more responsive, but to make the Helpline more effective GFC will need to create an incentive system to en-courage technicians to contribute. The incentive may be, but should not necessarily be limited to, financial. It could, for example, be a system that depends more on personal pride than financial rewards. If technicians propose solutions to problems, the engineers in Detroit could test them, and the solutions that work would be posted on the GFC Website and Helpline, acknowledging the individual technician who made the original contribution. In this case, the technicians' motivation would stem from their wish to be identified as the person who solved a difficult problem and to be acknowledged for their skill.

Improve Distance Education System logistics. Though DES is an effective vehicle for broadcasting the training programs, it would be considerably improved with some simple logistical changes.

The daily routine in a dealership is hectic and unpredictable, which makes class planning and scheduling difficult. Currently there is a two- to three-week lag time between signing up and taking a class because it takes that much time to ship the workbook to the dealership. If the workbooks were available on the Internet, the employees could download the latest version and print them whenever they were needed. If an afternoon looked slower than usual, a manager could pull off one of the employees to take a class without disrupting the normal work of the dealership or overburdening the other employees who have to cover for the student-employee. Having this flexibility would, of course, require an Internet-accessible computer and printer in the training room.

The phone-in aspect of the programming, though adding an important and much-appreciated spontaneity to the classes, also needs to be improved. Far too much time is wasted when calls from the participants do not go through. In addition to technical improvements to reduce or eliminate this problem, e-mail or live chat could be introduced as an additional channel between the dealership and the class host. This would allow participants to ask questions or make short comments, and would also allow the "just testing" messages to go through, but not interfere with the rest of the programming. Obviously this, too, would require providing e-mail access in the training room.

Continuing to keep the programs live is important because it gives the programs a freshness and sense of immediacy that helps maintain the learner's attention, but live programming also means that scheduling is much more restricted and inflexible. Alternative ways of delivering the programs to the dealerships could be explored. Managers do worry that if the training is not done during the work hours, it simply would not happen, and they are often rightfully reluctant to force employees to train on their own time. But there are situations when employees would like to take extra classes on their own time, and for them, having copies of the classes on VHS or DVD would be a welcome addition. To make this a viable solution, GFC will need to ensure that the cost of training is not transferred to the individual employee.

Investigate non-IT solutions. Though IT can certainly provide a medium for people who are geographically separated to learn and communicate, non-IT solutions are also available. GFC could look to the parts managers groups as an administrative model for transmitting concerns or suggestions back to the head office. Local events, both formal and informal, could be encouraged, which would increase informal communication between dealerships and their employees. In addition, the printed surveys that the head office mails out to dealership employees must allow for a higher level of anonymity. Mail-in survey forms sent to employees should not have the name of the dealership on it or have a tracking identification number, if candid responses are desired.

CONTENT

Once a robust and easy-to-use communication system is in place, the next step is to consider the information that could and should be flowing between Detroit and the dealership employees.

Clarify type of information. GFC needs to specify what type of information it would like from the dealerships, who needs it, and which employees can provide it. It has already developed systems that allow technicians to share their knowledge with the Detroit engineers, but more encouragement is needed. In contrast, there are very few systems in place for parts employees, service advisors, or salespeople to collaborate or share their knowledge. And because there is no history of communicating with Detroit, it will be more of a challenge to start the process. These employees not only will require some kind of incentive, but also will need very specific examples of what type of information is needed.

The types of information that GFC will be looking for are lessons learned and best practices that could be shared with other employees. Lessons learned often involve revealing mistakes that were made and suggesting how to avoid them in the future. The employee has to first admit that he or she (or someone else in their group) made a mistake before they can suggest ways of avoiding it. In any culture, but especially in this one, individuals, departments, and dealerships are reluctant to admit mistakes. Even if individuals are willing to be candid about their mistakes, their supervisors may not be. Best practices, on the other hand, are a far more neutral or even positive concept because they do not require attributing blame, and they focus on solutions and devising a better way of accomplishing a task.

To obtain the information it wants—whether it be lessons learned or best practices—GFC will have to effect a fundamental shift in the corporate culture. Not only will GFC and dealers have to refrain from punishing individuals or departments that admit errors, they will have to be flexible and accepting of the information that they receive. Some may be negative or unhelpful, but in order to encourage that flow of information the Detroit managers will have to gracefully accept any and all suggestions. It would be counterproductive to ask for help and then either dismiss it or redefine the problem so that the solution is no longer relevant. In addition to being open and accepting of this new flow of information, the Detroit managers must be seen as acting upon it.

GFC will also need to offer greater reward and recognition to those employees who do volunteer information, suggest a new idea, or come up with a fix for a problem. Given the existing culture of the dealership, where success is measured in financial terms, it is unlikely many employees will become "learners" and "sharers" without some kind of meaningful reward, which could involve cash, gift certificates, or redeemable points.

Increase formal learning. In spite of the manufacturer's emphasis on learning, the amount of training that dealership employees are actually required to do is not excessive. It may seem counterintuitive, but demanding more in terms of formal learning, not less, and making it more rigorous, might encourage the employees to take it more seriously.

GFC could offer incentives for dealership employees to take more classes on their own time. The classes could be shortened to an hour and put on VHS, DVD, or as streaming video. Participants could watch it on their own time and take an online test to verify that they learned the material. Again, some type of financial reward could be considered.

In addition to increasing some of the DES training, GFC and its dealerships will also need to rethink their definition of learning. For a learning community to exist, the flow of information must be two-way, and it cannot be strictly hierarchical—the roles of teacher and student must blur. Training then becomes not just a matter of designing courses and broadcasting content, but of facilitating participation and supporting learning communities—a much more difficult and demanding undertaking, but ultimately more effective.

Train Detroit employees. The two-way communication that GFC wishes to cultivate with the dealers obviously requires a sender and a receiver. This means that not only does GFC have to think about how to encourage dealership employees to contribute their experience, it has to pay equal attention to training its own head-office employees to listen and to regard the dealers as valuable business partners, rather than second-class citizens. And not only do they have to gracefully accept the information given to them, they have to act upon that information and give regular feedback to the dealerships.

Listen through unconventional channels. If the head office wants to learn about dealership employees' concerns, it does not necessarily need to create a new online discussion area. It could begin simply by finding out what current and former employees are saying on existing "alternative" Websites. Though this information can be raw and often overwhelmingly negative, the head office will certainly find out what is on the employees' minds.

For example, at one point most of the discussion on one Website focused on complaints about the flat rate. The technicians were claiming that the rate (time allotted for each job) had been slashed in the past year, which meant that their salaries had also been drastically reduced. As a result, they were frustrated and bitter, and claimed that vehicle safety was being undermined. The situation seemed to be reaching a crisis level. Then there were reports that the rate to replace or repair one particular part had been inexplicably halved. One week later, the head office recalled that part. Because dealerships must accept and fix all recalls, they obviously had a large influx of this one particular repair. By reducing the rate, GFC only had to pay half the normal amount to the dealerships for each job, and as a result the technicians only received half their usual salary for this work. Whether the story is true is not so much the point. The head office needs to be aware of such situations and should take immediate steps to clarify or correct them. Doing nothing is the worst of all scenarios.

Create online discussion. Creating a discussion site for all of the manufacturer's dealership employees could be beneficial for both the head office and the dealerships. Though anonymity is not usually recommended as a way to develop a sense of community online, this group may be an exception. Given the culture and the fear of reprisal, providing the option of anonymity would help relieve the wariness that so many employees feel and would allow them to express their opinions more candidly. Certainly not all of the site should be anonymous. Participants do need to take both responsibility and credit for their contributions, but there could be places on the site where optional anonymity would be beneficial.

CULTURAL AND SOCIAL, AND ECONOMIC
AND WORK ENVIRONMENTS

Information technology may be able to improve and facilitate the transmission of information (that is, lower the transaction cost) but as we have seen, the problems dealers and their employees face are more than simply the inability to send or receive information. Providing the means and the information will be challenging, but changing the underlying economic, work, social, and cultural environments will be not only the most important, but also the most difficult. Making changes at a structural level requires a fundamental shift in the work culture as well as in individuals' assumptions and attitudes. It will be a very difficult task.

Offer PCs to dealership employees. GFC could first start by making a grand and generous goodwill gesture toward the dealerships and their employees to symbolize that they are co-workers and partners. An example of another grand gesture was GFC's announcement in the late 1990s that it was offering to every one of its employees, from factory workers in India to auto designers in Michigan, their own high-speed desktop computer, a color printer, technical support, and unlimited Internet access for $5 a month. The offer, however, was limited to GFC employees—dealership employees received nothing. Extending this type of generous offer to the dealers would go a long way in generating goodwill and emphasizing that they are all in the business together. And not only would this help reduce some of the resentment that has built up over the years, but as an important secondary benefit it would also provide the means for every dealership employee to communicate directly with the head office—exactly what it professes to want.

Improve customer communication. Both the Detroit office and the dealerships could significantly improve communication with customers, which would result in not only more satisfied customers who might be more willing to return

TABLE 5.2
The benefits and costs of proposed improvements

PHYSICAL ENVIRONMENT

Action	Benefits	Costs
Improve quality and prominence of training rooms	Increased emphasis on the importance of learning and training	Increased expense

MEDIUM

Action	Benefits	Costs
Provide e-mail and Internet access	Increased communication between GFC and dealerships and between dealerships	Moderately expensive
	Allows head office to contact employees directly, bypassing dealership management	Dealership management may see it as a threat and weakening of their position
	Allows dealership employees to contact head office directly, bypassing supervisors and regional field office	Dealership management may see it as a threat and weakening of their position
Allow dealers to use off-the-shelf equipment	Less expensive for dealers	
Share cost of new information technology	Less expensive for dealers	More expensive for manufacturer
	Generate goodwill with dealers	
	Dealers may be more receptive to proposed changes	
Develop applications using commercially available software	Less expensive for dealers and manufacturer	
Develop applications in consultation with dealership staff	Better, easier-to-use software	Low cost
	Dealership staff will feel that head office managers are listening to them and care about their input	
Improve technician's Helpline	Better communication with technicians Technicians feel that they are contributing and are valued Detroit engineers receive their expertise	Some increased investment

Action	Benefits	Costs
Improve DES logistics by providing workbooks online	Greater scheduling flexibility in the dealerships	Will need Internet access in the training room
Provide e-mail and Internet access to supplement the phone call-in part of the program	Improved communication between hosts and participants More engaging programs	Will need Internet access in the training room
Move some training to the Internet, CDs, and DVDs	Training possible at home or off-site	Employees will need access at home; extension of an already long workday (that is, the cost of training is transferred to employees from dealership)
Encourage informal and formal local meetings and events	Greater communication between dealerships and employees	Dealers may fear other dealers would steal their employees
Allow anonymity in printed surveys	More candid opinions	

Action	Benefits	Costs
Clarify the type of information desired from dealership employees	Increased communication and understanding of Detroit needs	
Be open to criticism and accepting of mistakes	Increased and more candid flow of information	Change in corporate culture required
Offer incentives or rewards (financial or otherwise) for suggestions and fixes	Increased flow of information	Some expense
Increase training and learning for dealership employees	More learning	Longer work days, but there may be compensation with incentives and rewards
Train GFC Detroit employees to receive information	Better reception of information flow from dealerships	Requires a change in attitude on the part of Detroit employees
Listen to existing (non-GFC) channels of information	Quickly understand the major problems that dealerships face	
Create online discussion areas for GFC dealership employees	Increased understanding of the daily problems faced by dealership employees	Creates an obligation to help resolve the problem

TABLE 5.2 *(continued)*

ECONOMIC, WORK, CULTURAL, AND SOCIAL ENVIRONMENTS

Action	Benefits	Costs
Grand gesture: extend program of providing computers, printers, and Internet access to include all dealership employees	Symbolize that dealers are partners with GFC	Expensive
	Provide at-home access for increased training and communication	
	Generate goodwill with employees	
Improve customer communication	Improve working conditions for staff	Modest expense
	Generate customer goodwill and trust	
Experiment with creating a "new" type of dealership	Small-scale experiments rather than all dealerships	Expensive Legal challenges possible
	Opportunity to work under very different conditions; that is, local competition is absent	
	Lessons learned could be applied more broadly to traditional dealerships	

to the dealership in the future, but a less adversarial work atmosphere for the dealership employees.

Research tells us that customers develop trust (and will more likely become repeat customers) when they are treated fairly and politely and when their problem is resolved. Dealers could begin to use information technology to develop this trust. For example, service departments could start by letting the customers know what is expected of them and what kind of information will be required when they bring in their vehicles for repair or maintenance. A printed sheet or a Website (in several languages) could pose all the questions that a service advisor would normally ask, including asking for the vehicle identification number, model, and year. It could also include the questions required for diagnostics, such as whether the problem occurs early in the morning, when going up a hill, only when the vehicle turns left, and so on. Receiving these questions before arriving at the dealership service department would give customers time to gather more detailed and accurate information, which would be provided to the service advisors. It would also send the important message to the customer that GFC and the dealership want to fix the problem as quickly and effectively as possible the first time.

A Website or printed brochure for each dealership can also be used to give customers an idea of how much a typical repair will cost. Customers fear an unpleasant surprise when they bring in their vehicle. Publicizing the price, or at least a reasonable range, will help customers form realistic ex-pectations, and it reassures them that they are being treated equitably (an-other essential ingredient in building trust). It also indicates to the customer that the dealer might be interested in long-term customer relations, not just one-time, short-term profits.

Creating a Website for a dealership is obviously the responsibility of the individual dealer, but GFC did begin offering assistance to dealers in late 1999 by offering to create and host individual sites. An even greater help to dealers would be to create informational sheets, such as the list of questions asked by service advisors, and make them available online. Dealers could then either copy or make simple links to the page rather than create their own versions. GFC could also help the dealerships take advantage of new developments in computer and communication technology by offering DES classes on topics such as designing, creating, and hosting a Website, as well as how to use it effectively as a marketing tool.

Change the ground rules. Some of the most difficult and intransigent ob-stacles to improving the flow of information between the Detroit office and the dealerships involve the basic structure of the work environment. The pace of work, the competitive atmosphere within and between dealerships, a salary system that rewards the quantity rather than the quality of sales, a constant and unwavering focus on profits that discourages innovation and experimentation, and an often negative and adversarial atmosphere all con-spire against communication and the sharing of knowledge. Making any changes to this tangle of disincentives will be difficult indeed.

Instead of tweaking the system, GFC could be daring and experiment in a way that would have previously been considered impossible or outrageous. For example, GFC could choose a relatively small and contained geographic area, buy out the local dealerships (at a very generous price), and begin to experiment with the underlying structure and the economic, work, social, and cultural environments. However, given the dark history and fear that dealers have of manufacturers taking over sales, GFC would have to be very careful in its selection and terms. The advantage of this approach is that the dealerships in an area would become partners rather than competitors, and employees would receive a good salary rather than a commission. The new structure would have to be approached as an ongoing experiment—by both the manufacturer and the dealers—and as a way of discovering a better way of selling and servicing vehicles. Not every new technique or process would be successful, but honesty in admitting failure would be its strength and the foundation of its credibility. Of course dealers would be encouraged to visit, see for themselves, make suggestions, and learn, and any relevant lessons learned from this experiment could then be applied more broadly to the rest of the dealerships. It could be the model for creating a learning environment that is so badly needed in this industry.

It certainly would not be an easy undertaking, given the commitment and effort needed to overcome the wariness, suspicion, and fear of the dealers, the inertia of the industry, and the very strong franchise laws in many states protecting dealerships and preventing the auto manufacturers from selling vehicles. If it could happen, the industry would have a wonderful opportunity to experiment with the existing system and integrate changes once they have been proved to work. It would give them a chance to design a new type of organization and to explore how a learning community might develop in a less competitive environment.

CHAPTER SIX

Conclusion

The automobile industry has changed significantly over the past fifteen years. Today's vehicles are much more complex, and the differences between different makes are becoming minimal. The quality of vehicles has improved, the competition is intense, and profits from the sales of new cars are down. Customers are changing as well. They are less loyal to any particular brand, they are becoming much more discriminating consumers, and they are willing to use the Internet to gain information about vehicles and the sales process, and even to purchase vehicles online. Within the dealership, the sales department is no longer the primary economic engine, and the service department is developing a much more important role. Building customer loyalty by ensuring customer satisfaction is the new mantra. It is a time of change for the manufacturers and their dealerships, and they are struggling to adapt to this new environment.

In such a rapidly changing and somewhat unpredictable environment, the sharing of knowledge, communication, and learning has become more important than ever. GFC had already developed a satellite system for delivering training programs to its dealerships, and it wanted to expand the use of the system, in addition to increasing the use of other computer and communication technologies, to help create a learning organization—a group that constantly shares knowledge and information. The Detroit managers, however, perceived that the dealerships were rather unenthusiastic about information technology and resistant to the idea of becoming a learning organization. They wanted to understand why the dealers and their employees were reacting this way and what could be done about it.

Systematic observation of the work environment and work practices revealed that there are overwhelming forces working against GFC's desire to increase learning and communication. Implementing change will be very difficult given the sheer size of the corporation, its culture, and the historically adversarial relationship between the head office and the dealerships. The obstacle to becoming a learning organization is not backward dealers and individuals who reject technology, as GFC originally assumed. Nor is the obstacle arrogant and insensitive GFC staff in Detroit who do not understand the work of dealerships. In fact, both the dealerships and GFC employees are reacting in a quite rational and reasonable way given the circumstances of their work. The real culprit is the structure of the industry, the culture, the business practices, and the work environment—all of which stifle communication, learning, and the use of information technology. These are structural and institutional problems that cannot be changed lightly or easily.

But can these changes be made? In spite of the many obstacles, the situation certainly is not hopeless. The parts departments are already at least partially successful at communicating with GFC and each other, and their pay structure, atmosphere, and participation in a wider community all contribute to making them a community of practice. If it is possible to cultivate these conditions in one workgroup within dealerships, is it reasonable to expect it of the others? Can the other workgroups be more like the parts departments?

There are actions that GFC can take to improve the flow of information between Detroit and the dealerships and between dealerships. For example, providing greater access to the Internet and being explicit about the information that is needed would help improve the exchange of information. But to create a true learning organization that constantly shares information, more fundamental changes in the existing structure and business practices are needed. Though changes in the economic, work, social, and cultural environments are more likely to create long-term positive results, they are also the most difficult to implement.

Without changing the fundamental structure of the business, the chances of GFC becoming the learning organization that it aspires to be are low. Indeed, without these changes it is difficult to even image the company continuing to thrive. Making relatively minor changes such as providing the means to share information will help, but it will not be enough to initiate fundamental change because the problems that prevent the flow of information are much deeper. For example, the salespeople will never share their knowledge, no matter how much hardware and software they have, until they are no longer in active competition with each other. And they will never be able to treat the customers as GFC would like as long as they are encouraged and rewarded by GFC to push up the price and sell as many vehicles as possible. Customers will never feel fully comfortable in the showroom until they can trust that the price they pay is a fair one and that others are paying the same price. And no dealership employees will ever feel motivated to communicate and share information if they fear punishment or reprisals.

The real question is, Is GFC willing and able to make the changes? Is the goal of increasing learning and communication worth the long and hard process required? Perhaps GFC hoped that becoming a learning community was as simple as the enthusiasts portrayed, and any changes would be relatively simple and painless. It is quite possible that GFC may choose to stay with a hierarchical top-down structure and the status quo in terms of work practices and relationships—as dysfunctional as they may appear to those outside the industry. They could reason that the system has certainly worked in the past; manufacturers and dealers have had great financial success with the existing system, and it is hard to argue with success. But it could be so much better. Imagine a workplace where employees enjoyed coming to work, where employees were motivated, committed, and enthused—and, most unimaginable of all, where the customers were treated fairly and respectfully, and actually did not dread buying a new vehicle or getting it serviced.

And therein lies the limitation of design. We can study a workplace in great detail and gain valuable insight into how and why the employees work as they do. We can imagine and design new ways of doing our work, new ways of relating to each other, and new ways of understanding our role and contribution in the workplace. But design cannot make the changes. This lies solely in the hands of GFC and its dealerships. Whether they have the will, the energy, the perseverance, the imagination, and the courage—in short, the leadership—is a question that only GFC can answer.

An important lesson demonstrated by this case study is that, similar to many workplaces, employees within the dealerships were not a monolithic group and should not be treated as such. For example, technicians, service advisors, parts employees, and salespeople operate in quite distinct work environments; their assumptions and work practices differ, as do their attitudes and approaches to information technology, learning, communication, and community. At one end is the sales department, which resists both learning and sharing of knowledge. In the middle are service advisors and technicians. The advisors may be relatively willing learners and are the communicators within the dealership, but they have little or no contact with GFC. The technicians are relatively willing learners and have the means to communicate, but they do not always take advantage of the means they do have to exchange information with the engineers in Detroit. And at the other end are the parts employees, who cooperate with their competitors and manage to transmit their concerns to GFC through an administrative group they have created. Because the groups are so distinct, it is essential to tease apart and understand these differences in order to design viable solutions for each group that will enable learning and communication to take place. One size will not fit all.

Different lessons can also be derived from this case study of GFC dealerships depending on the discipline or field. To the social anthropologist, the most important lesson would likely be the influence of social roles and identity and how that influence effects the flow of information. To the economist, the lesson would be the importance of creating the right financial incentives for each of the dealership groups. The computer scientist would emphasize the need for well-designed software and easy-to-use operating systems to encourage learning communities. Those in organizational management would likely view the most significant lesson as the importance of having proper managerial policies and structures in place. And those from other disciplines would surely take still other slightly different perspectives.

Each of those perspectives would be correct, but each would also be slightly incomplete. The most important lesson gained from this study is that the complex set of issues faced by GFC, or any workplace or organization, must be viewed through multiple lenses rather than a single one; limiting the perspective to a single discipline or field will give a focused but narrow view of the issues, and design can play a significant role in widening that view. Design not only provides an overarching multidisciplinary approach that can embrace multiple perspectives, but through reflective and careful study of the problem it can offer practical and effective solutions for increased learning, working, and collaborating.

Designing a better environment, policy, or organization also underscores the importance and need for a subtle and fine-grained understanding of the social, technical, organizational, economic, and physical conditions that make up the workplace. Only with broad insight into work practices can the technology and associated policies be crafted to match the different needs and attitudes of the individuals and organization. As Van Maanen and Barley (1984) pointed out, there is a significant difference between organizational and occupational theory—one looks at the work from the perspective of the employer in terms of coordination, authority, and workflow, while the other focuses on individuals in an attempt to understand why they behave as they do. Clearly, the financial, management, and organizational requirements of the employer must be considered; it is a necessary but not sufficient condition. The most successful way to create learning organizations is to look closely at the employees' work practices, their attitudes, and the environment in which they work, and then design effective solutions based on that context.

And finally, we need to remind ourselves that the problems and obstacles faced by GFC are not unique and they are not an aberration. GFC is a very large corporation in an even larger industry. Its experience is similar to the other automobile manufacturers, but more important, it is similar in many ways to almost any firm, institution, or organization, public or private, large or small. If any workgroup, whether it be an academic institution, a restaurant chain, an architecture firm, or an international development organization, looked closely at its own work practices and work environment, it would likely find some uncomfortable similarities to GFC. Perhaps these might not be quite as extreme or on the same scale, but many if not all of the same barriers to becoming a learning community would be there. If greater sharing of knowledge is the goal, *any* organization would benefit from the process of learning from its work and designing a work environment that truly supported learning and communication within the workplace.

Notes

1. For example, see Peter Rowe's *Design Thinking* (1987: 48–54) for a description of the many theories and models.

CHAPTER TWO

1. The earliest automotive dealers apparently were not highly competent, because so many "were drawn from three unpromising groups: nephews and favorites of the well-to-do, those who had failed in other businesses, and bicycle repairers" (Rubenstein 2001: 252).

2. There are dozens of books on the history of the automobile industry and the men who built it, but most focus almost exclusively on the manufacturing process, management, and labor issues at the factory, and very little on dealerships or the sales and servicing of vehicles. Richard Tedlow (1990) proposes that the reason so little attention has been paid to this topic is because the sale of cars was seen as unimportant. The demand was so great that marketing was little more than an informality. The topic is not completely ignored however. Those books that do cover the history of dealerships include Robert Genat's *The American Car Dealership* (1999); *America's Auto Dealers: The Master Merchandisers* by Art Spinella and others (1978); and Jay Ketelle's *The American Automobile Dealership: A Picture Postcard History* (1988). Good general histories that cover dealerships include James Flink's *The Automobile Age* (1988) and *The Car Culture* (1975), and John Rae's *The American Automobile Industry* (1984). For a perspective on marketing, see Richard Tedlow's "Putting America on Wheels: Ford vs. General Motors" in *New and Improved: The Story of Mass Marketing in America* (1990), and Thomas Dicke's "From Agent to Dealer: The Ford Motor Company, 1903–1956" in *Franchising in America: The Development of a Business Method, 1840–1980* (1992). For a reference that lists almost every book written on any aspect of the automobile industry, see Michael Berger's 2001 *The Automobile in American History and Culture*.

3. Not all manufacturers were quite so ruthless, however. During this period, General Motors was known to be somewhat more conciliatory toward its dealers and made an effort to adjust production (May 1989: 311–312).

4. Dodge is owned by Chrysler, but not all dealers sell all makes made by the manufacturer.

5. For example, dealerships spent a record $7.75 billion on advertising in 2005. On average, a dealership spends a total of $360,225 annually, with over half spent on newspaper advertising and the rest divided between radio, television, and other media. This works out to spending an average of $457 on advertising per new vehicle sold (NADA 2006).

6. All data, except where noted, come from *NADA Data 2006*, Industry Analysis Division of the National Automobile Dealers Association (NADA). The data are published annually in *AutoExec Magazine* as well as on NADA's Website at www.nada.org.

7. Though there are some dealers who are women, the vast majority are men.

8. One example is the policy that states that parts should not stay on the shelf longer than six months. In theory this a good idea, but in New England, where weather can vary so much and extend into other seasons, dealers often keep some parts in stock for longer periods of time just in case their customers require them. Because the policy does not take into account differences in geographic location, dealerships in this region are penalized for keeping the parts on the shelf for too long.

9. The plan to consolidate dealerships is going much slower than planned because of tightened franchise laws in major states such as Texas and because some dealers feel that the manufacturer is forcing them to sell (Muller 1999). Dealers are fighting back, and it is not clear if Ford and GM will succeed (Ball 2000).

10. Increasing customer loyalty in the service department has not been an easy task. According to a 1998 report by J.D. Power and Associates titled *Service Usage and Retention Study*, 46 percent of customer expenditures for service goes to nondealer providers, and about half of the defections from dealerships are attributable to customer dissatisfaction caused by the amount of time taken to service the vehicle and the need to return to the dealership because of unsatisfactory work. The study found that most customers use nondealer providers because of convenience, location, amount of time to get the work done, good past experience, and competitive price.

CHAPTER THREE

1. Some dealerships are experimenting with or considering returning to the non-appointment system.

2. Many dealerships use odd times such as 7:05, 7:20, or 7:35 to reinforce the idea that these are precise times, not estimates, and customers are expected to be there on time.

3. Though dealerships are not usually located near public transportation, they rarely offer to loan vehicles to customers. Many dealerships have a driver who will drop off a customer, but these usually are not regularly available or convenient.

4. The dispatcher's job is a good example of what Lucy Suchman (1994) calls "articulation work," which she defines as continuous effort to bring together discontinuous elements into work configurations. She offers the work of the traffic controller in the operations room of an airport as an example. This person must coordinate across multiple settings and interdependent activities to accomplish the orderly arrival and on-time departure of an airline's flights.

5. Most parts are charged to the repair order, except for stock items such as brake cleaner, windshield fluid, grease, and coolant, which come out of general supplies.

6. Part of this vignette was originally published in "Information Technology and Skill Requirements: Examples from a Car Dealership" in *Die Zukunft computergestützter Kfz-Diagnose* (Beamish, Levy, and Murnane 2002, pp. 151–154).

7. The total invoice cost of the car is due to the manufacturer, payable by the dealership, when the vehicle is ordered, not when it is sold. Because car dealerships (or any retail operation, for that matter) must have an inventory on hand, they must borrow money from the bank to pay for that inventory. The manufacturer pays for financing and maintenance for the first ninety days the vehicle is on the lot in the form of a quarterly check called "holdback." After those first ninety days, the dealership dips into its own pocket, and into its own profit, to finance the car. This amount is "invisible" to the consumer because it does not appear on the dealer invoice (except in the case of Mitsubishi Motors, where the manufacturer allows dealers to charge the customer directly for the holdback). Therefore, the dealership is guaranteed a profit even if it sells a car at cost (if the car is sold within ninety days) (Source: www.edmunds.com/edweb/holdback_list.html).

8. One also suspects that the customer's gender played a part in the dealership's reaction. If a tall man who wore shoes with leather heels had made the same complaint, it is unlikely that his concern would have been labeled as "unreasonable" and dismissed quite as quickly.

9. A medium-large parts department would carry an inventory with approximately 18,000–20,000 lines of parts, worth about $350,000.

10. Female technicians are very rare.

11. If the problem requires major work or an expensive part, he will have the service advisor check with the vehicle owner before any work is begun.

12. In addition to *Consumer Reports* (www.consumerreports.org), some of the common Websites for sales and vehicle information are Microsoft Autos (www.carpoint.msn.com), AutoSite (www.autosite.com), Autobytel (www.autobytel.com), and AutoWeb.Com (www.autoweb.com). Consumer information can also be found at Intellichoice (www.intellichoice.com), Kelley Blue Book (www.kbb.com), and Edmunds (www.edmunds.com). Even the National Highway Traffic Safety Administration

has a site (www.nhtsa.dot.gov) that informs consumers if there are any recalls on their vehicles.

CHAPTER FOUR

1. For a visual record of the automobile dealership's evolution during the twentieth century, see Jay Ketelle's *The American Automobile Dealership: A Picture Postcard History* (1988).

2. Apparently the physical and visual separation also served a strategic purpose in the past. Norval Hawkins, a commercial and general sales manager for Ford from 1907 through 1919 urged dealers to not erect glass partitions between their showrooms and their repair shops "lest customers be reminded of all the things that could go wrong with their Model Ts" (May 1990: 246).

3. The most recent version, however, does note, "Many new cars have several on-board computers, operating everything from the engine to the radio. Some of the more advanced vehicles have global positioning systems, Internet access, and other high-tech features integrated into the functions of the vehicle. Therefore, knowledge of electronics and computers has grown increasingly important for service technicians" (Bureau of Labor Statistics 2004).

4. See Attewell 1990, Barley 1988, Vallas 1990, and Spenner 1990. In particular, see Levy and Murnane's *The New Division of Labor: How Computers Are Creating the Next Job Market* (2004) for an overview and discussion of the conceptual issues of skills and IT in the workplace.

5. See, for example, Graham and Marvin 1996 and 2001.

6. See Lucy Suchman's *Plans and Situated Actions* (1987) and Jean Lave's and Etienne Wenger's *Situated Learning* (1991) for a fuller description of the meaning of "situated," which in essence blurs the line between the artifact and the environment. Context is everything, making technology and the environment interdependent and inseparable.

7. Orlikowski (1995) proposes four distinct types of reactions to technology adoption. At one end of the spectrum is "technological shunning," when users choose not to use the technology at all. Next is "technological skepticism," when users doubt technology's benefit and so only half-heartedly attempt to use it. Then there is "technological substitution," when users use the technology to perform tasks that had previously been done in other ways. And finally there is "technological exploration," when users have greater interest in the technology but usage can be episodic if they are concerned about the consequences of using the technology within their institutional context.

8. For example, see Allard 1998, Lai and Guynes 1997; Julien and Raymond 1994; and Saleh and Wang 1993.

9. To be fair, though the dealers often bitterly complained about the expense, they often did not have to pay for the complete system. The manufacturer often paid for at least part of the equipment.

10. As with all databases, there are the usual problems with spelling errors, typos, and different ways of writing a name. Though different entries may all refer to the same person, the database counts them as separate customers, resulting in the loss of important customer information and repair history. Many dealerships use the customer's phone number rather than a unique identifier, which can cause further confusion because numbers change and many people use multiple phone numbers (home, office, cell).

11. Every vehicle is identified by a number that is used to track warranty repair history.

12. Newer vehicles can have over two hundred sensors.

13. Correspondence courses and the development of a reliable postal system marked the beginning of distance education. Caleb Philips of Boston is thought to be the first person to offer distance education. In 1728 he began mailing weekly shorthand and accountancy lessons to students living in rural areas. Though a satellite system may seem a long way from Philips's shorthand lessons, one of the common threads of distance education has been the enthusiastic embrace of new technologies, whether it be the postal system, radio, television, or the Internet (Mood 1995: 1–2).

14. Though the majority of the literature looks at the concept of learning organizations very positively, some authors, such as Marsick and Watkins (1999), Armstrong (2000), and Driver (2002), also see its potential for greater control and exploitation of employees.

15. See Sun (2003) for a review of the concepts from a linguistic point of view.

16. As Tsang (1997: 80) states, most talk about learning organizations is maddeningly abstract or vague and perpetually falls short on the specifics.

17. Yang, Watkins, and Marsick (2004) and Goh (2001) have gone so far as to develop measurements for learning organizations.

18. Snell goes so far as to say that failure to achieve the characteristics of learning organizations reflects a lack of ethical practices, principles, and virtues (Snell 2001: 323), but Salaman (2001) counterargues that the lack of attainment of a learning organization has less to do with morality than it does with its conflict with the realities of organization at the structural and cultural levels.

19. The assumption behind promoting learning organizations is that it will enable companies to anticipate and respond to change quickly, resulting in strategic and financial benefits. For example, see Baldwin, Danielson, and Wiggenhorn 1997; Lipshitz, Popper, and Oz 1996; Redding 1997; and Simonin 1997. Managers, however, have sometimes made the mistake of assuming that learning will automatically improve performance. As Tsang (1997: 78) points out, organizational learning is neither a necessary nor sufficient condition to guarantee financial or strategic advantage in any business.

20. Before Lave and Wenger, Van Maanen and Barley had developed the very similar and overlapping concept of "occupational communities," which they define as a group of people who consider themselves to be engaged in the same sort of work;

whose identity is drawn from their work; who share a set of values, norms, and perspectives; and whose social relationships meld work and leisure. Occupational communities create and sustain relatively unique work cultures consisting of task rituals, standards for proper and improper behavior, work codes surrounding relatively routine practices, and, for the membership at least, compelling accounts attesting to the logic and value of these rituals, standards, and codes (1984: 287). Van Maanen and Barley developed the notion of an occupational community to understand why people behave as they do in the workplace, and developed the framework to concentrate on the meaning of work for those who do it.

21. Lave and Wenger call this type "legitimate peripheral participation."

22. In the shop, Detroit management has pressured GFC dealerships to accept certification by introducing a policy of not paying for certain warranty repairs unless they are done by a technician certified for that particular system.

23. To prepare for the broadcasts, instructors undergo an eight-hour orientation session and then spend another eight hours of rehearsal time for every one hour of airtime in order to keep timing and technical glitches to a minimum.

24. Employees lose their certification if they do not complete their required courses by December 31.

25. Because they are not in direct competition with each other, it is to their advantage to have competent and well-trained co-workers.

26. The way service advisors are trained is a good example of Lave and Wenger's "legitimate peripheral participation."

27. This is also true of the service advisors. GFC wants to make the consumer more powerful in symbolic ways, such as by offering greater cheerfulness and an obliging attitude. Because this is what "non-expert" or low-status employees such as servants are supposed to do, the service advisors who consider themselves expert and superior find this difficult to accept. In their eyes, a show of respect or deference would lower their status.

28. Social ties are the links that bind individuals to other individuals. Granovetter (1973) differentiated between strong and weak social ties. Strong ties are maintained through frequent and emotionally intense communication, often entailing the sharing of confidences over time, and the establishment of reciprocity between parties. Weak ties are maintained through less frequent and less emotionally intense communication and do not require or encourage the sharing of confidences or the establishment of strong reciprocities. Weak ties are maintained among extended family members, co-workers not central to an individual's task domain, and everyday acquaintances made in connection with work, social activities, and mutual friendships. This theory suggests that relative strangers and their weak ties can be positive and can offer advantages over friends and colleagues in obtaining useful information.

29. See, for example, Coate 1997; Harasim 1995; Hiltz and Turoff 1993; and Sproull and Kiesler 1991.

30. Dealers, quite understandably, hate being put in the embarrassing position of being caught off-guard and finding out about a manufacturer's recall from their customers, rather than from the head office.

31. The threat is only a local one, however. Only the dealers located within driving distance would be considered rivals. The farther away another dealership is, the less of a competitive threat it becomes.

32. In spite of these rather positive characteristics, apparently a psychological test administered to top automotive salespeople in 1996 found that a top salesperson is "inflexible, doesn't have much empathy, can't reason abstractly, and is not particularly open or thorough" (Rubenstein 2001: 251).

33. A 2000 issue of *The New Yorker* included an article called "How to Sell Cars," about a new General Motors salesman learning to sell cars. He is upset when an elderly customer to whom he sold an expensive car is not treated fairly. The story ends with another salesman telling him, "You can't be a salesman, Benny, . . . and expect to go to heaven" (Cheever 2000).

34. Unlike twenty years ago, today there is no longer any mention of computers substituting or replacing technicians. In 1984, Ferron and Kelderman predicted that "played to the limit in the creation of an automobile, new technologies could theoretically eliminate the need for highly trained mechanics. Computers should be able to tell anyone with a rudimentary knowledge of mechanics what is wrong and how to fix it. GM is already headed in this direction with its '800 number' central computer which handles diagnosis of tricky problems the dealer mechanic cannot solve" (1984: 70). Practical experience has proved that as helpful as the new technology is, it is no threat whatsoever and will never substitute for a trained and experienced technician. In fact, knowledgeable and talented technicians are more in demand than ever.

35. None of the dealers or managers interviewed said that this had ever happened to them personally, but in their minds it was clearly a very real possibility and an ever-present danger.

36. No dealer or manager ever expressed a desire or conscious intention to produce this kind of negative environment. They could always identify when their own ideas were quashed by their bosses, but none ever admitted to doing the same to their own subordinates.

37. See Smith and Meiksins (1995) for an overview of how engineers' attitudes affect the generation and diffusion of best practices. They claim that, unlike American engineers, their Japanese and Swedish counterparts tend to regard manual workers as co-workers and not subordinates without input into decision making.

38. Not all industries share information with each other, however, and employees are careful about what they share. What and how much information is shared usually depends on the degree of competition between the involved firms, the availability of alternative information sources, whether the information relates to a domain in which the firms compete, the likelihood that the other firm will reciprocate

information, the value of the transferred information to the receiver, and the technical expertise of the information receiver.

39. Customer satisfaction is a major concern for dealers, not simply because they want satisfied customers, but because when certain vehicles are in high demand and supplies are tight, the manufacturer will often allocate scarce cars based in part on customer satisfaction ratings, which are derived from surveys sent to every recent new-car buyer.

40. The work done by auto technicians has many similar, but not identical, characteristics to that of Julian Orr's (1996) Xerox technicians. Orr found a triangular relationship between the machine, the customer, and the technician, whereas in a dealership the customer is a more distant actor who is only heard through the description on the service advisor's repair order. Also see Bonalyn J. Nelsen's *The Nature and Implication of Technological Change and the Rise of a Service Economy: Observations from the Field of Automotive Repair* (1997) for a discussion of opacity and transparency in automobile repair shops. She argues that because automobile technicians combine the characteristics of both expert and nonexpert work, many organizations manage this cultural anomaly by promoting either opacity (systematically separating customers from the technicians) or transparency (encouraging interpersonal contact between them).

41. These salaries are in 2006 dollars.

42. A medium-large parts department with four to five full-time employees can provide the parts for fifteen to twenty technicians, field two hundred telephone calls a day, serve walk-up customers, unload delivery trucks, and answer questions on pricing and availability for the service advisors.

43. Salaries in the Northeast range from $40,000 to $60,000 per year for a fifty-hour week (in 2006 dollars), but a highly experienced and skilled technician could make $72,000 to $85,000 a year, though this is not typical. Experienced and specialized technicians who prefer to be paid hourly earn in the $30-per-hour range plus benefits while less skilled and experienced technicians, who handle most routine work such as tuneups and oil changes, earn approximately $10 to $12 per hour.

44. The salaries of salespeople are usually based on commission, so what they earn is a direct reflection on the number of cars they sell. Salespeople in the Northeast can earn $50,000 a year (2006 dollars), or they can make $90,000, depending on how good they are. New salespeople usually average $35,000 to $40,000 a year, though a few can get up to $60,000 or $70,000. Successful salespeople can sell ten to fourteen cars per month, which would give them a good, but not extravagant annual salary.

45. A medium-large dealership would sell approximately 120 to 140 cars per month. On a slow day, the sales department would sell 2 to 3 cars, and 7 to 8 on a busy day. Sales managers estimate that for every 4 people who walk in the door, they'll make a sale to one person, which means that in a medium-sized store about 120 to 150 people walk into the showroom per week.

46. Indeed, the Saturn Corporation is well known for their now famous "no-hassle, no-haggle sales policy."

References

Allard, Mark. 1998. Overcoming Cultural Barriers to the Adoption of Object Technology. *Information Systems Management* 15(3): 82–85.

Argyris, Chris, and Donald A. Schön. 1978, 1996. *Organizational Learning: Theory, Method, and Practice.* Reading, MA: Addison-Wesley.

Armstrong, Helen. 2000. The Learning Organization: Changed Means to an Unchanged End. *Organization* 7(2): 355–361.

Attewell, Paul. 1987. Big Brother and the Sweatshop: Computer Surveillance in the Automated Office. *Sociological Theory* 5: 87–99.

Attewell, Paul. 1990. What Is Skill? *Work and Occupations* 17(4): 422–448.

Ayres, Edward. 1970. *What's Good for GM . . .* Nashville: Aurora.

Baldwin, Timothy T., Camden Danielson, and William Wiggenhorn. 1997. The Evolution of Learning Strategies in Organizations: From Employee Development to Business Redefinition. *The Academy of Management Executive* 11(4): 47–58.

Ball, Jeffrey. 2000. Auto Dealers, Fearing That Detroit Will Hog the Web, Fight Back. *The Wall Street Journal,* May 10, 2000, A1, A12.

Barley, Stephen R. 1988. Technology, Power, and the Social Organization of Work: Towards a Pragmatic Theory of Skilling and Deskilling. *Research in the Sociology of Organizations* 6: 33–80.

Barlow, John Perry. 1994. The Economy of Ideas: A Framework for Rethinking Patents and Copyright in the Digital Age. *Wired* 2(3): 84–90, 126–129.

Beamish, Anne, Frank Levy, and Richard J. Murnane. 2002. Information Technology and Skill Requirements: Examples from a Car Dealership. In *Die Zukunft computergestützter Kfz-Diagnose,* ed. N. S. Felix Rauner and Georg Spöttl. Bielefeld, Germany: W. Bertelsmann.

Berger, Michael L. 2001. *The Automobile in American History and Culture.* Westport, CT: Greenwood Press.

Boland, Richard J. Jr., and Fred Collopy. 2004. Design Matters for Management. In *Managing as Designing,* ed. R. J. Boland Jr. and F. Collopy. Stanford, CA: Stanford University Press.

Bradach, Jeffrey L. 1998. *Franchise Organizations*. Boston: Harvard Business School Press.

Braverman, Harry. 1974. *Labor and Monopoly Capital: The Degradation of Work in the Twentieth Century*. New York: Monthly Review Press.

Browne, Joy. 1973. *The Used-Car Game: A Sociology of the Bargain*. Lexington, MA: D.C. Heath.

Buchanan, Richard. 2004. Management and Design: Interaction Pathways in Organizational Life. In *Managing as Designing*, ed. R. J. Boland Jr. and F. Collopy. Stanford, CA: Stanford University Press.

Bureau of Labor Statistics. 2004. *Occupational Outlook Handbook, 2004–2005 Edition, Automotive Service Technicians and Mechanics*. Washington, DC: U.S. Department of Labor.

Bureau of Labor Statistics. 2007. *Occupational Outlook Handbook, 2006–2007 Edition, Automotive Service Technicians and Mechanics*. Washington, DC: U.S. Department of Labor. (www.bls.gov/oco/ocos181.htm, accessed July 09, 2007).

Cheever, Benjamin. 2000. How To Sell Cars. *New Yorker* (April 24 and May 1, 2000): 136–158.

Coate, John. 1997. Cyberspace Innkeeping: Building Online Community. In *Reinventing Technology, Recovering Community: Critical Explorations of Computing as a Social Practice*, ed. P. E. Agre and D. Schuler. Norwood, NJ: Ablex.

Constant, David, Lee Sproull, and Sara Kiesler. 1999. The Kindness of Strangers: The Usefulness of Electronic Weak Ties for Technical Advice. In *Shaping Organization Form: Communication, Connection, and Community*, ed. G. Desanctis and J. Fulk. Thousand Oaks, CA: Sage.

Critchlow, Donald T. 1996. *Studebaker: The Life and Death of an American Corporation*. Bloomington: Indiana University Press.

Cultum, Gordon A. 1956. *An Automobile Dealership*. B. Arch. thesis, Department of Architecture, MIT, Cambridge, Massachusetts.

Dertouzos, Michael. 1997. *What Will Be: How the New World of Information Will Change Our Lives*. New York: HarperCollins.

Dicke, Thomas S. 1992. *Franchising in America: The Development of a Business Method, 1840–1980*. Chapel Hill: The University of North Carolina Press.

Dilworth, Robert L. 1996. Institutionalizing Learning Organizations in the Public Sector. *Public Productivity & Management Review* 19(4): 407–421.

Driver, Michaela. 2002. The Learning Organization: Foucauldian Gloom or Utopian Sunshine? *Human Relations* 55(1): 33–53.

EDC (Education Development Center). 1998. *The Teaching Firm: Where Productive Work and Learning Converge*. Newton, MA: Center for Workforce Development, Education Development Center, Inc.

Edwards, Richard. 1979. *Contested Terrain: The Transformation of the Workplace in the Twentieth Century*. New York: Basic Books.

Etheredge, Lloyd S. 1976. *The Case of the Unreturned Cafeteria Trays: An Investigation Based Upon Theories of Motivation and Human Behavior.* Washington, DC: American Political Science Association.

Ferron, J., and Jake Kelderman. 1984. *Betting on the Franchise: Car and Truck Retailing into the 1990s.* McLean, VA: National Automobile Dealers Association.

Flink, James. 1975. *The Car Culture.* Cambridge, MA: The MIT Press.

Flink, James. 1988. *The Automobile Age.* Cambridge, MA: The MIT Press.

Fowler, P., I. García-Martín, N. Juristo, and L. Levine. 1995. A Prototype Knowledge-Based Tool for Software Engineering Adoption and Implementation. In *Diffusion and Adoption of Information Technology,* ed. K. Kautz and J. Pries-Heje. London: Chapman & Hall.

Garrick, John. 1998. Informal Learning in Corporate Workplaces. *Human Resource Development Quarterly* 9(2): 129–144.

Garvin, D. A. 1993. Building a Learning Organization. *Harvard Business Review* 72(4): 78–91.

Gates, Bill. 1996. *The Road Ahead.* New York: Penguin Books.

Genat, Robert. 1999. *The American Car Dealership.* Osceola, WI: MBI Publishing Company.

General Motors Corporation. 1948. *Planning Automobile Dealer Properties.* Detroit, MI: Service Section, General Motors Corporation.

Gephart, Martha A., Victoria J. Marsick, Mark E. Van Buren, and Michelle S. Spiro. 1996. Learning Organizations Come Alive. *Training & Development* 50(12): 35–45.

Goh, Swee C. 2001. The Learning Organization: An Empirical Test of a Normative Perspective. *International Journal of Organizational Theory and Behavior* 4(3&4): 329–355.

Graham, Stephen, and Simon Marvin. 1996. *Telecommunications and the City: Electronic Spaces, Urban Places.* London: Routledge.

Graham, Stephen, and Simon Marvin. 2001. *Splintering Urbanism: Networked Infrastructures, Technological Mobilities and the Urban Condition.* London: Routledge.

Granovetter, M. 1973. The Strength of Weak Ties. *American Journal of Sociology* 78(6): 1360–1380.

Grudin, Jonathan. 1990. Groupware and Cooperative Work: Problems and Perspectives. In *The Art of Human-Computer Interface Design,* ed. B. Laurel. Reading, MA: Addison-Wesley.

Guthrie, K. Kendall, and William H. Dutton. 1992. The Politics of Citizen Access Technology: The Development of Public Information Utilities in Four Cities. *Policy Studies Journal* 20 (Winter 1992): 574–597.

Harasim, Linda M. 1995. Networlds: Networks as Social Space. In *Global Networks: Computers and International Communication,* ed. L. M. Harasim. Thousand Oaks, CA: Sage.

Herring, Susan C. 1996. Gender and Democracy in Computer-Mediated Communication. In *Computerization and Controversy: Value Conflicts and Social Choices.* Second edition, ed. R. Kling. San Diego: Academic Press.

Hiltz, Starr Roxanne, and Murray Turoff. 1993. Social and Psychological Processes in Computerized Conferencing. In *The Network Nation. Revised Edition.* Cambridge, MA: The MIT Press.

Hislop, Donald. 2003. The Complex Relations Between Communities of Practice and the Implementation of Technological Innovations. *International Journal of Innovation Management* 7(2): 163–188.

Huber, George P. 1996. Organizational Learning: A Guide for Executives in Technology-Critical Organizations. *International Journal of Technology Management, Special Issue on Unlearning and Learning for Technological Innovation* 11(7/8): 821–832.

J.D. Power and Associates. 1998. *Service Usage and Retention Study.* Agoura Hills, CA: J.D. Power and Associates.

Julien, Pierre-André, and Louis Raymond. 1994. Factors of New Technology Adoption in the Retail Sector. *Entrepreneurship Theory and Practice* 18(4): 79–90.

Ketelle, Jay. 1988. *The American Automobile Dealership: A Picture Postcard History.* Amarillo, TX: Jay Ketelle Collectables Inc.

Kirby, Robert Sean. January 15, 1998. *Automotive Mechanics. 1998–1999 Occupational Outlook Handbook.* Washington, DC: U.S. Department of Labor, Bureau of Labor Statistics. Stats.bls.gov/oco/ocos181.htm, accessed December 11, 1999.

Lai, Vincent S., and Jan L. Guynes. 1997. An Assessment of the Influence of Organizational Characteristics on Information Technology Adoption Decisions: A Discriminative Approach. *IEEE Transactions of Engineering Management* 44(2): 146–157.

Langley, Ann, and Jean Truax. 1994. A Process Study of New Technology Adoption in Smaller Manufacturing Firms. *Journal of Management Studies* 31(5): 619–652.

Lave, Jean, and Etienne Wenger. 1991. *Situated Learning: Legitimate Peripheral Participation.* Cambridge: Cambridge University Press.

Lawson, Bryan. 1997. *How Designers Think: The Design Process Demystified.* Oxford: Architectural Press.

Levy, Frank, and Anne Beamish. 1999. *Information Technology and Customer Relationships.* Cambridge, MA: Massachusetts Institute of Technology.

Levy, Frank, and Richard J. Murnane. 2004. *The New Division of Labor: How Computers Are Creating the Next Job Market.* Princeton, NJ: Princeton University Press.

Lipshitz, Raanan, Micha Popper, and Sasson Oz. 1996. Building Learning Organizations: The Design and Implementation. *The Journal of Applied Behavioral Science* 32(3): 292–305.

Marr, Paul R. 1985. *The Automobile Dealership Service Industry: An Operations Management Analysis.* Master of Science thesis, MIT, Cambridge, Massachusetts.

Marsick, Victoria J., and Karen E. Watkins. 1990. *Informal and Incidental Learning in the Workplace.* London: Routledge.

Marsick, Victoria J., and Karen E. Watkins. 1999. Looking Again at Learning in the Learning Organization: A Tool That Can Turn into a Weapon! *The Learning Organisation* 6(5): 207–211.

May, George S. 1989. Marketing. In *The Automobile Industry, 1920–1980*, ed. G. S. May. New York: FactsOnFile.

May, George S. 1990. Norval Abiel Hawkins. In *The Automobile Industry, 1896–1920*, ed. G. S. May. New York: Bruccoli Clark Laymann.

Meredith, Robyn. 2000. Autobytel Plans to Sell Cars Directly Over the Internet. *The New York Times*, January 24, 2000.

Mohr, Lawrence B. 1982. *Explaining Organizational Behavior.* San Francisco: Jossey-Bass.

Mood, Terry Ann. 1995. *Distance Education: An Annotated Bibliography.* Englewood, CO: Libraries Unlimited.

Moore, Gary C., and Izak Benbasat. 1991. Development of an Instrument to Measure the Perceptions of Adopting an Information Technology Innovation. *Information Systems Research* 2(3): 192–216.

Muller, Joann. 1999. Meet Your Local GM Dealer. *Business Week*, October 11, 1999, 48.

NADA (National Automobile Dealers Association). 1973. *Dealership Organization and Management.* Midland, MI: Northwood Institute.

NADA (National Automobile Dealers Association). 1992. NADA Data 1992: Economic Impact of America's New-Car and New-Truck Dealers. *Automotive Executive.*

NADA (National Automobile Dealers Association). 2003. NADA Data 2003: Economic Impact of America's New-Car and New-Truck Dealers. *AutoExec Magazine.*

NADA (National Automotive Dealers Association). 2006. NADA Data 2006: Economic Impact of America's New-Car and New-Truck Dealers. *AutoExec Magazine.*

Nardi, Bonnie A., and Vicki L. O'Day. 1999. *Information Ecologies: Using Technology with Heart.* Cambridge, MA: The MIT Press.

Naughton, Keith. 1996. Revolution in the Showroom. *Business Week*, February 19, 1996, 70–76.

Negroponte, Nicholas. 1995. *Being Digital.* New York: Vintage Books.

Nelsen, Bonalyn J. 1997. *The Nature and Implications of Technological Change and the Rise of a Service Economy: Observations from the Field of Automotive Repair.* Ph.D. thesis, Cornell University, Ithaca, New York.

Orlikowski, Wanda J. 1995. *Action and Artifact: The Structuring of Technologies-in-Use.* Cambridge, MA: Sloan School of Management, Massachusetts Institute of Technology.

Orlikowski, Wanda J., and Debra C. Gash. 1994. Technological Frames: Making Sense of Information Technology in Organizations. *ACM Transactions on Information Systems* 12(2): 174–207.

Orr, Julian E. 1996. *Talking About Machines: An Ethnography of a Modern Job.* Ithaca, NY: ILR Press.

Parasuraman, A., Leonard L. Berry, and Valarie A. Zeithaml. 1991. Perceived Service Quality as a Customer-Based Performance Measure: An Empirical Examination of Organizational Barriers Using an Extended Service Quality Model. *Human Resource Management* 30(3): 335–364.

Pickering, Jeanne M., and John Leslie King. 1995. Hardwiring Weak Ties: Interorganizational Computer-Mediated Communication, Occupational Communities, and Organizational Change. *Organization Science* 6(4): 479–486.

Pool, Ithiel de Sola. 1983. *Technologies of Freedom: On Free Speech in an Electronic Age.* Cambridge, MA: The Belknap Press.

Pyka, Andreas. 1997. Informal Networking. *Technovation* 17(4): 207–220.

Rae, John B. 1965. *The American Automobile.* Chicago: The University of Chicago Press.

Rae, John B. 1984. *The American Automobile Industry.* Boston: Twayne Publishers.

Redding, John. 1997. Hardwiring the Learning Organization. *Training & Development* 51(8): 61–67.

Reger, Guido, and Dorothea von Wichert-Nick. 1997. A Learning Organization for R&D Management. *International Journal of Technology Management, Special Issue on R&D Management* 13(7–8): 796–817.

Rowe, Peter. 1987. *Design Thinking.* Cambridge MA: The MIT Press.

Rubenstein, James M. 2001. *Making and Selling Cars: Innovation and Change in the U.S. Automobile Industry.* Baltimore: The John Hopkins University Press.

Salaman, Graeme. 2001. The Learning Organization: Fact or Fiction? *Human Relations* 54(3): 343–359.

Sale, Kirkpatrick. 1995. *Rebels Against the Future: The Luddites and Their War on the Industrial Revolution: Lessons for the Computer Age.* Reading, MA: Addison-Wesley.

Saleh, Shoukry D., and Clement K. Wang. 1993. The Management of Innovation: Strategy, Structure, and Organizational Climate. *IEEE Transactions on Engineering Management* 40(1): 14–21.

Sanford, Charles L. 1983. "Woman's Place" in American Car Culture. In *The Automobile and American Culture*, ed. D. L. Lewis and L. Goldstein. Ann Arbor: The University of Michigan Press.

Schrader, Stephan. 1992. Informal Information Trading Between Firms. In *Transforming Organizations*, ed. T. A. Kochan and M. Useem. New York: Oxford University Press.

Seiders, Kathleen, and Leonard L. Berry. 1998. Service Fairness: What It Is and Why It Matters. *The Academy of Management Executive* 12(2): 8–20.

Senge, Peter. 1990. *The Fifth Discipline: The Art and Practice of the Learning Organization.* New York: Doubleday/Currency.

Senge, Peter. 1994. *The Fifth Discipline Fieldbook: Strategies and Tools for Building a Learning Organization.* New York: Doubleday/Currency.

Senge, Peter. 1996. Building Learning Organizations. *IEEE Engineering Management Review* 24(1): 96–104.

Simonin, Bernard L. 1997. The Importance of Collaborative Know-How: An Empirical Test of the Learning Organization. *Academy of Management Journal* 40(5): 1150–1174.

Sligo, Frank. 1996. Disseminating Knowledge to Build a Learning Organization. *The International Journal of Human Resource Management* 7(2): 508–520.

Smith, Chris, and Peter Meiksins. 1995. The Role of Professional Engineers in the Diffusion of "Best Practice" Production Concepts: A Comparative Approach. *Economic and Industrial Democracy* 16(3): 399–427.

Snell, Robin Stanley. 2001. Moral Foundations of the Learning Organization. *Human Relations* 53(3): 319–342.

Spenner, Kenneth I. 1990. Skill: Means, Methods, and Measures. *Work and Occupations* 17(4): 399–421.

Spinella, Art, Beverly Edwards, Mo Mehlsak, and Larry Tuck. 1978. *America's Auto Dealers: The Master Merchandisers.* Van Nuys, CA: Freed-Crown.

Sproull, Lee, and Sara Kiesler. 1991. *Connections: New Ways of Working in the Networked Organization.* Cambridge, MA: The MIT Press.

Stambler, Howard V. 1957. Employment Outlook for Automobile Mechanics. In *The Occupational Outlook.* Washington, DC: U.S. Department of Labor, Bureau of Labor Statistics.

Stamps, David. 1998. Learning Ecologies. *Training,* January 1998, 32–38.

Suchman, Lucy. 1987. *Plans and Situated Actions: The Problem of Human-Machine Communication.* Cambridge, UK: Cambridge University Press.

Suchman, Lucy. 1994. *Supporting Articulation Work.* Paper read at International Conference on Women, Work and Computerization: Breaking Old Boundaries, Building New Forms, at Manchester, United Kingdom, July 2–5, 1994.

Sullivan, Ray Anthony, ed. 1962. *The Automobile Dealer and His Employees: A Management Guide to Assist New Car and New Truck Dealers in Building and Retaining an Efficient and Progressive Organization.* Washington, DC: National Automobile Dealers Association.

Sun, He-Chuan. 2003. Conceptual Clarifications for "Organizational Learning," "Learning Organization" and "a Learning Organization." *Human Resource Development International* 6(2): 153–166.

Tedlow, Richard S. 1990. Chapter 3: Putting America on Wheels: Ford vs. General Motors. In *New and Improved: The Story of Mass Marketing in America.* New York: Basic Books.

Throckmorton, Robert Bruce. 1973. *Boundary Roles and Occupational Integration: An Examination of the Automobile Salesman.* Ph.D. thesis, Department of Sociology, University of Washington, Seattle.

Toffler, Alvin. 1980. *The Third Wave.* New York: William Morrow.

Tsang, Eric W. K. 1997. Organizational Learning and the Learning Organization: A Dichotomy Between Descriptive and Prescriptive Research. *Human Relations* 50(1): 73–89.

Vallas, Steven Peter. 1990. The Concept of Skill. *Work and Occupations* 17(4): 379–398.

Van Maanen, John, and Stephen R. Barley. 1984. Occupational Communities: Culture and Control in Organizations. In *Research in Organizational Behavior,* ed. B. M. Straw and L. L. Cummings. Greenwich, Conn.: JAI Press.

Verespej, Michael A. 1998. Formal Training: "Secondary" Education? *Industry Week*, January 5, 42–43.

Ward's Dealer Business. 2003. Internet Flexes Muscle. *Ward's Dealer Business.*

Wenger, Etienne. 1998. *Communities of Practice: Learning, Meaning, and Identity.* New York: Cambridge University Press.

Wenger, Etienne, Richard McDermott, and William M. Snyder. 2002. *Cultivating Communities of Practice: A Guide to Managing Knowledge.* Boston: Harvard Business School Press.

Westrum, Ron. 1991. *Technologies and Society: The Shaping of People and Things.* Belmont, CA: Wadsworth.

Whipp, Richard, and Peter Clark. 1986. *Innovation and the Auto Industry: Product, Process and Work Organization.* New York: St. Martin's Press.

Yang, Baiyin, Karen E. Watkins, and Victoria J. Marsick. 2004. The Construct of the Learning Organization: Dimensions, Measurement, and Validation. *Human Resource Development Quarterly* 15(1): 31–55.

Index